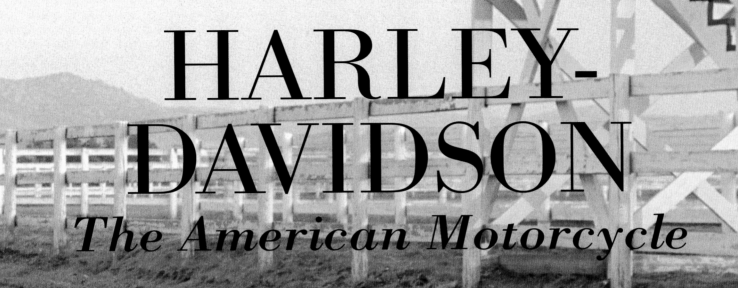

HARLEY-DAVIDSON

The American Motorcycle

ALLAN GIRDLER
PHOTOGRAPHY BY RON HUSSEY

MOTORBOOKS

This edition published in 2005 by Motorbooks, an imprint of MBI Publishing Company, Galtier Plaza, Suite 200, 380 Jackson Street, St. Paul, MN 55101-3885 USA

First published in 1992 by MBI.

Motorbooks titles are also available at discounts in bulk quantity for industrial or sales-promotional use. For details write to Special Sales Manager at MBI Publishing Company, Galtier Plaza, Suite 200, 380 Jackson Street, St. Paul, MN 55101-3885 USA.

ISBN-13: 978-0-7603-2448-6
ISBN-10: 0-7603- 2448-4

Printed in Hong Kong

Contents

Dedication and Appreciation

Most of the time, if I singled out one person who helped on a project, the other helpers would wonder why, and maybe even have their feelings hurt.

In this case, no fear. I dedicate this book to Armando Magri, who retired from his Sacramento dealership to spend more time with his collections, who has helped me every time I've asked for help and who cared about Harleys and history before most of us could spell them.

Plus, I'm happy to thank the owners of the bikes pictured; jurors Johnny Eagles, Mike Shattuck, Arlen Ness, Willie G. Davidson, Bud Ekins, and Jerry Hatfield; and not least Nancy, who accepted my proposal the day we photographed the Model 5 and who didn't mind postponing our honeymoon until the book was done and it was time to head for Daytona Beach.

Allan Girdler
Rainbow, California
February 21, 1992

Introduction

Putting some spin on one of life's better cliches, if Harley-Davidson history hadn't happened the way it did, it couldn't have been invented. If The Motor Company, as they call it in-house, hadn't grown from a backyard shed into an economic miracle and defender of the free market through its very own combination of guts, brains, luck, and occasional foolishness, nobody would have believed it. Even the checkout counter rags whose headlines brag about capturing Hitler or interviewing a space alien's two-headed children would reject the sagas of the Knuckle, the Sport, and the Hummer.

What we have here is truth that staggers fiction.

What we have because of that history and those sagas, is a celebration. This isn't a standard history of the company and its products, although there are facts included, as well as figures and a few conclusions.

Instead, this is an examination of the best and most important models from Harley-Davidson, an illustration by example, so to speak. We'll look at the models that best show how the company outlived its several hundred rivals on the scene in the early days, and how it got through the wars and depressions and invasions and fashions ever since, from its founding in 1903 until tomorrow, 1993, and the 90th Anniversary of what the Tribe (makers of the Indian Motocycle) used to call Hardly-Ableson.

Here we are, then, at the point where the reader is entitled to wonder exactly who made the picks, and how?

Begin with the jury foreman, aka me. I bought my first Harley in 1954, when I was seventeen and the bike, a VLH but not the precise VLH to be seen in due course, was twenty years old. I listened to all the stories and collected spare parts and managed not to hurt myself; indeed, I suspect now that I didn't get hurt mostly because the bike was so big and I was so skinny that I didn't take many chances.

In any event, I soaked up all the lore and believed all the tall stories and so I was the perfect guy to do a Buyer's Guide for used Harleys, which I did a few years back. (Check with the clerk at the parts counter if you missed it.) That book was followed by a history of racing Harley-Davidsons and then a detailed account of the XR-750, also to be honored later. Besides that, I have my very own XLH Sportster, an Evo edition, and a street-ready iron-barrel XR, a labor of several years.

So, your grease-stained author is brave and steeped in lore. What I am not, however, is foolish enough to tackle a project like this by myself.

The editorial "we" is used so that readers will think there's too many guys in the office to whip. With that in mind I enlisted help from a range of experts who truly know their stuff. The full list is in the acknowledgments, so for now just know that at least two of the jurors know everything about the teens, a couple more are experts on the bikes of the 1920s and 1930s, and then there are retired racers and one contemporary dealer. Most of the panel works outside the factory, in some cases competes with the factory, and one—who else but Willie G.?—has his name *on* the factory.

The selection procedure began with a philosophical approach. We set out to decide on the most significant models from H-D's ninety years. Careful here, because that doesn't always mean the most popular or the most economically successful; in fact, a couple of the models included were not accepted by the buying public, at least not then or in that form.

After that, there weren't any limits. We were open to road and racing models, big and small, works of art or (in my opinion, at least) downright homely.

We came up with a list of nominees, which I circulated among the panelists, most of whom wanted to add a model that had been left off the list, or (more often, I think) who were hopping mad about a mistake that had been included. If—as did happen—enough jurors yelled loudly enough, or marshaled enough facts, the offending nominee was removed from the list. And so it went until we reached a consensus—which you'll see in a few pages.

When the list was complete, Ron Hussey and I traveled to shows and swap meets and dealerships and even to Milwaukee, so we could borrow some time and help from the owners of the bikes. Most of our examples are in private hands, as I for one think they should be; it's much more fun when the one who rides the bike really knows and cares about it. (Each owner is listed with the lead photo in the bike's chapter, by the way.)

One last comment on the selection process. Some of the models chosen and celebrated here are exemplars, that is, the example shown represents the model as a model. When we used the XR-750 built and tuned by Bill Werner and ridden by Scott Parker, the defending national champ at the time, we used that team and machine to represent the XR-750 during the twenty years it has raced and won. Nothing personal, you could say.

Sometimes we picked an exact model, just the one year and only that year because that precise machine marked a moment in time, with consequences to come as a direct result of what the factory did with that model.

Teachers of writing (if that's not a contradiction—can writing really be taught?) say the toughest part of the job is writing the last line of the work. This is probably true. In that case, I'd like to give you my last line right now, along with my assurance that once you've read about Harley's Milestones, you'll understand why the most important thought, the secret of The Motor Company's success....

Harley-Davidson has *always* made motorcycles.

A Brief Harley History

Poet Randall Jarrell writes that when you look at the faded photos in the family album, to see those folks in their quaint suits and dresses, sporting muttonchop whiskers and muttonchop sleeves, is to realize that they knew as they stood before the camera that they were quaint, that their purpose on this earth was to be part of our pasts.

Jarrell was making a little joke that really isn't. It's easy to smile when we look back at the wobbly contraptions that ushered in the motoring age. How cute, we think, to include training wheels for the first motorcycle, the engine in a trailer towed by the two-wheeler it powers. How quaint.

But of course it was nothing of the kind.

It was creative engineering, dogged brilliance, and the slow accumulation of answers that only look easy *after* they were arrived at. Great leaps were mixed with cut-and-try at the turn of the century. Jarrell aside, the more I study the work of those pioneers, the more I doubt that I could have done nearly as well. And the same goes for you.

Which brings us to William S. Harley and Arthur Davidson, both of Milwaukee, Wisconsin, and childhood friends. They were young men in 1900, twenty and nineteen respectively. Harley worked as an apprentice draftsman and Davidson as a pattern maker at a fabricating plant.

The two young men were bicycle enthusiasts, a worldwide fad at the time, and were of course fascinated by the internal-combustion engine and the possibilities of putting motor and bicycle together. In 1900 they began building sort of a kit single-cylinder engine. They had it in a frame and running by 1903, then they built another. (In what would become tradition, the second one had a bigger engine.)

Late in 1903, young Harley and Davidson produced their first machine for sale. Like the prototypes and the first fifty or so examples made, it had a single-cylinder engine with atmospheric intake valve; that is, when the piston went down for the intake stroke, the valve was sucked open and when it started back up, the valve was compressed shut. There was one speed, forward, with drive by leather belt and with pedals for the steeper hills. The first examples used bicycle-style frames and wheels, with the wheels held rigidly in the frame. There was a bicycle-style brake in the rear hub, activated by pedaling backward. The machine would do 45mph or so, which must have been at least enough, and weighed less than 200lb.

William Harley and Arthur Davidson were joined by Arthur's brothers William A. and Walter and in 1907 the firm was incorporated as Harley-Davidson (it sounded better than the reverse, just as we wouldn't have liked Arrow-Pierce or Wesson & Smith).

This happened at a good time, a time when intelligent and energetic men could tackle a project like this with some hope of success. The official word has always been that the boys built those first bikes for themselves and went into business because the public liked the product. I think it's more likely that they hoped from the first that they could build a machine worth selling.

Which they could, and did.

But they weren't alone in their field. There were scores of people doing *sort of* the same thing. Except that most of the others didn't really know what they were doing. They hadn't done their homework, and simply bought an engine from one source, a frame from another, wheels and such from a third supplier, and so forth. They slapped the parts together and found a buyer or two and lasted about as long. Even the folks who knew better kept with the original formula, that of a bicycle powered by bolted-in internal combustion.

Harley-Davidson did it right from the start. First, the partners knew their stuff. Walter Davidson was a machinist (and by rare good fortune, a naturally gifted rider). William Harley was a draftsman who after the project began got an engineering degree. While an undergraduate, he designed the leading-link forks that graced Harley-Davidsons from then until 1949, and which, under the name Springer, were put back into production in 1988 on a limited-edition model.

Arthur Davidson turned out to have a commercial bent and realized early in the business that good dealers were as important as a good product. William Davidson, who never liked motorcycles all that much, knew people and how to lead them, even though his formal training was in toolmaking and metallurgy.

Next, they had resources. The Davidson and Harley families were prosperous members of the skilled working class. They had talent, ambition, energy, intelligence, and the willingness to work now in hopes of reward later. The families came through with operating capital. The Davidsons' dad built the shed that served as the original factory. As still another little stroke of fortune, an aunt, Janet Davidson, applied the red pin-striping to the first machines (which were black) and while she was at it, painted on the red and black badge which still symbolizes the Harley-Davidson Motor Company.

Well, the partners made their first sale in 1903. They'd learned from their prototypes that building a bicycle and adding an engine wasn't enough. They made the engines larger and the frames hell for stout. Working part-time, they made and sold two machines in 1904, eight in 1905, and fifty in 1906, all to the same general design because quality meant more than innovation. Production in 1907 totaled 150, and the partners knew it was time to incorporate and make The Motor Company a full-time proposition.

And now, it's time for the products to speak for themselves. . . .

Chapter 1

1909 Model 5

The One That Worked

To the current enthusiast, believing in a single-cylinder Harley-Davidson is a lot like believing in Peter Pan; that is, you gotta clap your hands a lot to make it come true.

But in 1909, the single was the Harley that worked. No matter how elemental a twin seems now, we can't escape the historical logic that says before the motorcycle could run, it had to walk.

With that in mind, take two good looks at the 1909 Model 5A. At first glance, it looks to be a bicycle, with pedals and drive chain on the right to supplement or even equal the sprockets, and leather belt on the left. And it's true that the Model 5—so called because 1904 was H-D's baseline year, marked zero so 1909 was the fifth model year—used a coaster brake, bought from Thor, a company which built its own motorcycles and sold parts to the little guy.

Look again, and there's more serious logic. While many of the other score or so of rivals in the field were building motorized bicycles, the founders at H and D realized they needed to supply transportation. The Harley-Davidson was created from the very first as a motorcycle, with frame and wheels and controls and so forth larger and stronger than the competition used, and okay, if that meant the Harley was heavier and cost more to build than the lighter jobs, so be it.

With that principle established, the early examples of the make were mostly conventional. The 1909 followed the patterns laid down in 1903 and 1904 by using the bicycle type, beefed as mentioned, frame, wheels, brakes, and controls. The engine was based on a design by De Dion, the French firm that pioneered the art, and was mostly a set of round crankcases with flywheels and connecting rod and cast-iron piston inside, and a sprocket for the belt on the outside.

The combustion chamber was offset to the bore of the cylinder, and the exhaust valve, lifted by a cam lobe in the timing case on the right, was next to the piston.

Intake was atmospheric: there was no cam lobe for the intake. Instead, the valve was above the exhaust valve. When the piston starts down in the intake stroke the suction pulls the intake valve open and mixed fuel and air are hauled into the cylinder. The piston starts back up and presto! the positive pressure pops the intake valve closed. It's held closed by the expansion during the power stroke and the upward motion of the piston during exhaust, then down goes the piston again, down pops the intake valve again, and the cycle repeats. Neat, easy, and simple.

When talking exhaust, we have a choice of nomenclature. The exhaust valve was below the intake valve, so the design was called intake over

The 1909 Model 5 typifies early Harley-Davidsons, in that it was big, strong, and powered by a single cylinder engine. Owner: Joy Baker, Vallejo, California.

This is a basic machine, with diamond frame, early versions of Harley's leading-link forks, and one speed forward. The tools—and battery, if so equipped—went in the case on the back of the central frame downtube.

The engine propels the machine by this leather belt. The lever above the pulleys is the clutch lever. Moving it tightens the belt on the pulleys.

Yes, the single-cylinder with pedal assist, the carbide-powered headlamp, and the leather belt look quaint. Nevertheless, technical progress was on the way.

What looks like a lovely old teapot is the headlamp. The lower section holds pellets which dissolve into carbide gas. The upper section is where the gas is burned to form enough light to be seen, if not actually permit the driver to see, at night.

exhaust, or IOE. The valves were off to one side of the cylinder bore, so the same design was called the pocket valve. In a poetic way, the valvetrain forms sort of an F shape, especially later with a pushrod and rocker arm, so the system has been known as the F head. But because IOE is the clearest and simplest term, we'll call it that from here on out.

Carburetion was achieved with a basic instrument, floats, and jets fed by gravity from the tank at the top frame rail. By 1909 everybody had seen the wisdom in Glenn Curtiss' invention of

16

A careful look reveals no valvetrain for the intake, which is opened and shut by atmospheric pressure. It worked, in the early days. The housing off the side of the crankcases drives and mounts the magneto and yes, those are bicycle pedals for starting the engine and sometimes giving a hand, so to speak, up hills.

Ignition is by magneto, an option in 1909 and more reliable than the baseline model, which had a breakable battery.

18

the twist-grip throttle, so that's what the Model 5 (and virtually all its peers) used. For the kids in the audience, note here that Harleys had their twist throttles in the right grip, Indians had theirs in the left grip, and there was no proven reason for picking either side. But—I speak from memory here—if you wanted your Indian to have controls like a Harley, you had to swap sides, which meant you reversed the action of the throttle—and wait till you borrowed a machine like that in heavy traffic!

The Model 5 oiling system was as automatic as the intake: When the piston moved up, the motion created a vacuum in the crankcase and that pulled a (hopefully) controlled dollop of oil into the cases, where it splashed around keeping things slick and cool until it was burned or leaked away. Total loss oiling, as they called it. It did the job, although now, with less stress on the antique engine and better oil in the tank, Marv Baker, operator of the Model 5 pictured, has to drain the unburned, unleaked oil out of the crankcase after the bike is ridden.

Speaking of total loss, the basic Model 5 came with battery-powered ignition, plug, points, and coil with juice from three dry-cell batteries. Right, the kind of battery that can't be recharged. Every so often you went to the hardware store and bought more batteries, right along with the oil.

This example has a new-for-1909 option, a magneto, producing its own electric charge and spark, driven off the timing case, same as for the single cam lobe. The magneto model was the 5A.

Reliable electrics, ready for the vibration and pounding that came with motorcycles of the day, were in the future. The headlight for the Model 5 was fueled from a tank into which one dropped pellets that formed carbide gas, as used in mines. It appears that the purpose of the headlight was more so that other road users would see you coming, instead of you seeing them.

Today, operating such a Spartan motorcycle seems nearly impossible. This one is owned by Joy Baker, of Vallejo, California, and was restored by her husband Marv, and is ridden by their son Randy. It's ridden *only* for special events.

That's because first, you get all the controls just right. The lever on the left side of the tank tightens the leather belt between engine and rear wheel sprockets. You ease off the belt and pump away on the pedals until you've got speed up, then pull back until the engine engages, catches, and fires. There's no clutch as such, no gearbox, and the belt doesn't like to be slipped. Tweak the throttle, spark advance, and tension lever until belt and pulleys are fixed together and away the 5A goes . . . in giant leaps. The engine runs best at 300 or so rpm. Yes, hundred, not thousand. The H-D single of 1909 displaced 30ci (cubic inches) and produced maybe 4bhp (horsepower). Randy Baker estimates top speed on today's paved roads at better than 45mph. That's the limit, he says, because the neat and simple automatic inlet valve only works to perhaps 500rpm. Faster than that, air pressure can't do the job. Dribbling fuel on your leg, Baker says, is nature's way of telling you that's fast enough.

Sounds like a grand toy, eh? It is, now. But the point here is, the Model 5, indeed all the Harley-Davidson singles, *worked*. The secret was in the integrity of the model and the maker. The first Harley-Davidson did 60,000-plus miles under its first five owners. Arthur Davidson went for the commercial business, pitching the product to mail carriers and others who needed a horse that didn't eat when it wasn't working. And in 1908, Walter Davidson rode a stock single to a perfect score in the nation's most important endurance run, this when endurance counted much more than speed or style.

The engineering was sound. The leading-link front suspension designed by Bill Harley while he was still a student was as good as any on the market. The big, strong Harley-Davidson, known as the Silent Grey Fellow because the founders were canny enough to put an efficient muffler on it, had a big, strong, understressed engine and drivetrain, a characteristic that the make would retain to the present day.

Yes, the single-cylinder with pedal assist, the carbide-powered headlamp, and the dawning-industrial-age leather belt look quaint. Nevertheless, technical progress was on the way.

Meanwhile, the single-cylinder with enough strength to satisfy six owners was laying the foundation for the next step, and it put Harley-Davidson into the motorcycle business, and in the black.

While many of the other score or so of rivals in the field were building motorized bicycles, H and D realized they needed to supply transportation.

Size of the front and rear pulleys dictated the gearing and thus the speed of the bike. The large rear and small front is because this engine is good for only 300rpm or so. Leather was a natural, as it was used in machine shops and factories of the day to do the same sort of work.

Next page
The Model 5 was obviously based on the bicycles of the day; the founders of the firm began as bicycle enthusiasts.

First spring suspension seat post, clutch. Dropped tanks to lower seat.

First rear stroke starter

HARLEY-DAVIDSON

1916

1909

1911

1909

Chapter 2

1909 Model 5D

The First V-Twin

Harley-Davidson didn't invent the V-twin. (Pause, for dramatic effect.)

Let me make that crystal clear because if there's one thing that identifies and distinguishes Harleys from lesser makes, for the True Believer and the station wagon driver alike, it's the rumble and roar, the sight of those massive cylinders jutting up and out of the crankcases and the frame. But Harley didn't do it first.

What really led to the V-twin concept was logic.

Consider the frames into which those pioneer bikers put engines. They used the design and example of what's formally known as the Safety Bicycle, with a diamond frame, so called because the frame is shaped like a diamond, or two triangles bisected. The triangle, incidentally, is nature's strongest shape.

So, if you locate the engine in the best place, the center of the leading triangle, the one with the narrow vee at the lowest point, you have a fine spot for a round crankcase and a lot of room above that just waiting to be filled with mechanical bits.

Now, the engine. Single cylinders naturally were the first choice. They could be bought from outside, or built in a modest shop with the aid of machinists and foundries, and because they used

the minimum number of parts, there were fewer things to break or fall off.

But in 1900, as it will be in the year 2000, there was a limit to how large you could make one cylinder, how much power you could get out of it, and how much stress you could feed into it. (True, the limits are higher than they were, but the fact remains.) Well before Harley met the Davidsons, engines of several cylinders had been used in motorcycles. Some were wondrous devices, for instance, the machine that had five cylinders set radially around the front hub and driving the front wheel. Some, the inline fours, were merely ahead of their time. But most of the examples used too much space and added too much weight to be a true advantage.

That's why the designers looked at those diamond frames, and then at the single-cylinder's crankcases. You have a round case, housing flywheels and a crankpin and driving, oh, a magneto and perhaps an oil pump. Let's say you tipped that solo barrel back a bit, so it's parallel to the rear frame tube—or even becomes the rear frame tube. Indian did that very thing. Or, you could tip the cylinder forward, parallel with the front tube.

You could cast in two base plates on the round set of cases. You'd have to make the cases stronger, thicker, and ready to take more pres-

Half great-grandfather, half black sheep, the 1909 5D was Harley's first production V-twin. Compare the profile of the twin with the single and you can't miss the logic of the experiment. Owner: Harley-Davidson Motor Company.

More logic, as the intake manifold fills the gap between the intake ports, and in the vee. The chrome caps atop each cylinder head are the housings for the springs that help close the intake valves.

The H-D founders knew the big single was the way to go while the motorcycle was still working toward becoming basic transportation. They also knew there'd be a time when one cylinder wouldn't be enough.

24

sure and vibration, but not twice as strong or heavy. You could put a second cylinder on that base.

The cases would need to be wider, but not by much, and there could be a second connecting rod on the crankpin, side by side or fork and blade, with one overlapping the other; Harleys have always been set up this way. You can juggle the valve gear and make one camshaft do all the work for both cylinders, ditto for the ignition and other components. What you end up with is double the number of cylinders and potential power, or an engine that runs smoother and stronger with less weight because there are smaller

Doubly classic, the vee is 45 degrees and the combustion chamber, spark plug, and valves are offset to the cylinder. Pocket valve, they said then, or Intake Over Exhaust (IOE).

25

The V-twin was mostly an enlarged version of the single of the same year, with oil and fuel tanks slung below the top rail and so forth. Lights were an option, not fitted to this survivor.

pulses and more of them. You've filled the vacant space, but haven't increased total size by nearly as much as you've gained: You've invented the V-twin!

As stated earlier, Harley-Davidson didn't do it first. It's such a logical improvement, so easy to conceive and execute, that nobody's really sure who did it first.

Nor were there many rules. The vee of the frame lent itself to a narrow vee on the cases, and there have been myriad executions of the theme, in 42, 45, 47, 52, and so forth degrees of included angle. The Americans, Germans, Swedes, and English all did it and they all did a good job.

There's a distinguishing feature or drawback, however; it's a matter of not quite achieving

symmetry. A four-stroke engine, of course, fires each cylinder every other revolution, so the V-twin fires the front, for instance, on the first round and the back barrel on the second, plus or minus the angle of the vee. The narrow angle means the pistons and rods are not quite in balance with each other and the staggered firing times, 315deg, 405deg, 315, 405, add to this; what you have is an engine that vibrates. Shakes. Blurs mirrors and tingles hands and puts toes to sleep and rattles parts loose. There are ways to reduce this and to disguise it (see chapter 21 on the FLT), but if it's a V-twin, that's how it will behave. And that's why we have flat-twins and

Pedals and chain get the machine under way at first. The tiny rear hub houses a bicycle-style coaster brake. On a good day this model would hit or approach 60mph, so even so small a stopper must have been welcome.

27

Fill 'em both up, they must have said with gas and oil tanks side by side. The plunger delivers a shot of lubricant when the going gets rough, as in up hills.

fore-and-aft twins and cross-the-frame fours and vertical twins and triples and all the other configurations that don't fit the diamond frame nearly as deftly.

Some introduction, eh? The H-D portion begins with the fact that the founders were intelligent and well-informed men. They knew what was being done next door and in other countries. They knew that the big (relatively) single was the way to go while the motorcycle was

still something that was working toward becoming basic transportation.

They also knew there'd come a time when one cylinder wouldn't be enough.

Exactly when this time came isn't clear. Official H-D historian David Wright says that a V-twin appeared in a show during 1907, but there are no extant photos. If there was such an event, the machine must have been a prototype because in 1909 there appeared, in the catalog and in

28

metal, a V-twin designated Model 5D; the Models 5, 5A, and 5C were variations on the single, as earlier described.

The twin was largely based on the single: same frame design, but longer and heavier. All the 1909 models used wire controls, such as the sleeve and inside strand wires routed through the handlebars for the throttle and spark controls, with brakes—bought from the Thor motorcycle company, on the rear wheel only. It had the same styling as the single, and the same options such as lights, which the Model 5D V-twin didn't get but the preceding single did. All the twins came with magneto ignition and 28in wheels, two features that were options for the single.

The V-twin engine was literally based on the single, with the cases getting some extra muscle and two places to bolt cylinders rather than one. The included angle was 45deg, as it's been for Harley-Davidson vees ever since. The twin shared cylinders with the single while the actual bore was 3.0in instead of $3^5/_{16}$in. Stroke for both engines was $3^1/_2$in, so the V-twin displaced approximately 50ci and the single 30ci; presumably the larger engine didn't need to be that much larger to do the job.

Heads were also in common, in design at least, with the intake ports in the center and the exhausts on the outside. One camshaft lobe took care of opening both exhausts and the intakes were atmospheric, pulled open by the partial vacuum created by the pistons' descent. IOE, as you'd expect, had the combustion chamber off to one side of the cylinder.

Beyond that, the 5D was basic. Like the singles from the same model year, it used pedals and chain to start things off: There was just the one speed, with drive via pulleys and a wide leather belt.

Obviously, the V-twin was supposed to provide more power and speed. And it did, in that the single developed around 4bhp (brake horsepower) and the twin gave somewhere between 6.5 and 7.0 plus change, depending on which source you trust. (Perhaps it's worth saying that none of the several sources is trying to trick anybody. Rather, we historians are pretty much

stuck with using the vague and sometimes romantic recollections that back then passed as official data.) Best estimates give the V-twin a top speed of 65mph, assuming a good day.

Best summation of the project is . . . not very good.

Not to play games, the V-twin wasn't a success. Not many were sold: The example shown is out of Harley-Davidson's own collection and as nearly anybody knows, there's only one other 1909 V-twin left intact in the world. They didn't sell because they didn't live up to expectations. Again, there are several versions of what went wrong.

First, the official word from inside is that the rest of the drivetrain wasn't up to the engine: The belt slipped. Just why they hadn't fitted the tensioner used on the single to the twins as well, the record doesn't say. But the smaller engine, that didn't have enough power to overcome the belt's grip, had a way to tighten the belt if needed. The twin didn't. Odd.

A second explanation is that the atmospheric intake valves had literally reached their limits, as mentioned in the preceding chapter, with engine speed and road speed held down to an estimated 500rpm. The pulleys on both look identical, which means they were geared nearly alike and that means the twin would have run out of road speed when the single did. That wasn't what the V-twin buyer had in mind.

As a clincher, the early H-D V-twins were notorious for being hard to start. Even the later models were this way, to the extent that at least one wife has persuaded her collector husband to swap the thing before bringing on a heart attack pedaling the V-twin around the show grounds.

Most likely, the V-twin suffered from all three of the above. In any event, the model was withdrawn from the 1910 line-up.

No prize for guessing that when the founders saw a good idea, they made it their own. In 1911 the V-twin went back into production, same general idea except that this time it came with a belt tensioner and with proper cam lobes and rockers and springs for the intake valves.

And the rest, as they say, is history.

If you locate the engine in the center of the frame's leading triangle, you have a fine spot for a round crankcase and a lot of room above that just waiting to be filled with mechanical bits.

Chapter 3

1916 Model J

No More Motor Bicycles

Now *this* is a motorcycle, which was the point of the Model J: No bicycle pedals, no leather belts. (The belt drive of course is an idea that will come again.) Owner: Custom Chrome Industries, Morgan Hill, California.

And now comes . . . the motorcycle.

Does that sound odd, seeing as H-D by 1916 had nearly a full generation and countless improvements in the sales and record books? Wasn't that first Harley-Davidson ridden 100,000 miles in its first ten years, and wouldn't that make it a real motorcycle?

Yes, but with reservations. The early Harleys were built more sturdily than their rivals but even so, they needed pedal assist for starting and for the occasional patch of really bad road. You had to restart when you stopped, which had to be a bother, and the leather belts weren't weatherproof: The factory's records show William Harley was aware the metal chain was more efficient right from the start, but wasn't willing to use chain drive until he'd come up with some sort of clutch that was better than the tensioner so easily fitted to the belt. That didn't take place until 1912, and the clutch was in the hub of the rear wheel.

The V-twin was introduced in 1909, as noted, then withdrawn from production for more work and was reintroduced in much improved form in 1911, as top of the line while the traditional single was the mainstay of the line.

That began to change. The eight-valve racers (see chapter 4 for details) were rare but refined. The engineering department learned a lot about cam and valve timing, carburetor size, and the like, and power became easier to get. The IOE engines benefited from this technical wizardry and by 1915 the basic details of the engine were in place, where they'd stay until 1929.

In 1916 the factory introduced a machine with all the improvements adopted since production began. It was a useful motorcycle, not a vestige of bicycle about it. And it serves here to show why and how Harley was catching Indian, the big guy.

The IOE engine displaced 61ci, a classic size even then, with bore slightly less than stroke. It was of course a 45deg vee, with the single carb in between the barrels and with fork-and-blade connecting rods. The valves were mechanically operated, with a lobe for each cylinder: Run the cam at half engine speed and you can use the same lobe with different rockers to open one valve when the piston's at the top, and a second rocker for when it's at the bottom.

There were no horsepower claims as such, but in 1915 the factory said they'd guarantee 11bhp because they'd seen as much as 16bhp on test. Power was no problem, as the bike would hit at least 60mph given hard pavement and a rider with no imagination.

Drive was by chains; one, the primary chain that connected the engine to the clutch and gear-

There are four pushrods now that the intakes have cam lobes and normal springs, but the 61ci V-twin comes from the same design department as the earlier engines did. The nickel-plated line coming from the vee and going into the timing case is the oil delivery, from the tank to the pump. There's a sight gauge so the careful owner can be assured oil is getting to the right place.

box, then the final drive chain, from gearbox to rear wheel.

The starter had made a final sort of evolution. First came the clutch in the hub, which let the rider pedal the engine to life without needing to prop the rear wheel off the ground. The 1916 Model J has a pedal that works backward, just like the lever on your dirt bike today. (It was called the step-start, a gentler and more accurate name than kick-start.) You keep one foot on the ground, leap into the air, and step down smartly and if all the controls are set right, the

engine starts up. That's how it was with a Harley in 1916, and so it would remain until 1965.

Just as important, the Model J had an oil pump. The system was still total loss: you put a few ounces into the cases, the oil gets burned away, you put in more. But when delivery was left to the owner with a pump, the owner tended to put in too much oil, which blocked the breathers, turned the engine into an air compressor, and overheated it. So the Model J had a pump that sent a tiny amount of oil into the sump by mechanical means, with the hand pump there

Previous page
Drive is by chain, an efficient
method that had to wait until
the product was as good as
the book said it would be, and
there's a luggage rack, proving
the point about transportation.

A genuine step-starter has
replaced the pedals and
pumping owner. There's a
linkage from lever crank to the
exhaust valves, which lifts the
valves from their seats and
reduces compression, and
resistance, when the engine is
being kicked over.

The headlight came from Klaxon, a name much better known for horns, and used gas, from the tank atop the bars, for illumination.

for an occasional extra supply, for a long hill perhaps. And there was a sight gauge so the owner could be sure the pump was on the job.

By 1916 electricity was becoming more technology than wizardry but as shown here, there were still those who preferred a magneto ignition with acetylene gas for the headlight: The lamp came from Prest-o-Lite—get it? An option for the Model J was a generator, complete with cutout so the battery didn't get cooked, and with a taillight that detached for use as a trouble light, no kidding. (The horn came from Klaxon. Ask your granddad.)

There was also an evolution of style with the Model J. The slab tank was replaced by tanks with more graceful curves, and the oil tank was moved from below the seat to within one of the twin tanks slung on the frame backbone, a feature Harley-Davidson has used to good effect ever since. The fenders are more fully valanced, that is, wrapped around the tire for more protection from mud and water. The machine *looked* competent, which was as useful on the showroom floor as being competent was on the road.

Suspension was rudimentary, with the rear wheel rigidly mounted and the front suspension, featuring once again the springer with leading links designed by William Harley, had only an inch or so of travel. In H-D's defense, it's worth mentioning that although some of the other outfits, Indian mostly, did offer rear suspension and more intricate front suspension, the designs

Next page
We already have evolution, with graceful curves modernizing the lines of the fuel tank, with fully valenced fenders to cope with rain and mud, while the 1916 obviously comes from the people who gave us the 1909s.

worked better in theory than on the road. So H-D stuck to what worked.

In summing up the Model J's history, there are three main points to be made.

First, the evolutionary nature of the road-going Harley-Davidson was an important factor. One of the stylist's toughest jobs then and now is to ensure the product looks like earlier examples from the maker and at the same time seems just a bit ahead of its time. To illustrate, compare the old and new Jaguar XJ6 sedans.

The 1916 Model J was new in 1916, and it looked it. At the same time, you can see the Silent Grey Fellow's genes every place on the bike.

Delivery lines for oil and gas are coiled because the metal was brittle and the engine vibrated, causing fatigue unless some flex was wound into the system.

37

The usefully narrow profile is marred a bit by the tank for the headlight gas and the horn, a Klaxon, which is the aggressively black object on the tank's left.

Suspension was rudimentary, with the rear wheel rigidly mounted and the front suspension, once again featuring the springer with leading links designed by William Harley, having only an inch or so of travel.

Second, great care was taken with every piece. The clutch is controlled by the rocker pedal at the front of the left footboard. The clutch isn't spring loaded, so it will stay disengaged at a stop. But just in case, there's a helper lever aft of the gearshift at the left side of the tanks, to keep the pedal where the rider wants it, and perhaps to free the left foot when the going's rough. The controls—for the valve lifter which reduces compression when starting, for instance—are routed all around, over and in between, in a series of intricate straight lines and pivots. No effort was spared to make things right.

And third, the Model J worked. Well sure, there was a long way to go, especially with lights, brakes, and suspension. But the third and most important factor was that this was a practical machine.

The Model J would take you where you wanted to go and bring you home. And if you looked a bit more bold and dashing than you actually had to be, well, that didn't hurt either.

Tanktop carried two caps for gas, one for oil, the gearshift gate, and the speedometer, with drive from the rear hub.

Chapter 4

1921 8-Valve Racer

Harley Wins 'em All

Racing wasn't part of the original Harley-Davidson plan; competition, surely. As noted, founders and family took part in reliability runs and other amateur contests when getting from A to B was an achievement, never mind how long it took. But for the first ten years of H-D's history, and in effect during the time competition grew from two guys headed the same direction on the same road to fully professional contests, Harley-Davidson had no team and took no official part in racing.

Then, probably for reasons of morale as much as money, the founders changed their minds and on July 4th (happy coincidence, surely), 1914, fielded a factory racing team. The venue was Dodge City, Kansas, by then a classic event; the distance was 300 miles around a dirt ring. H-D entered six machines, modified versions of the IOE 61ci twin. Four broke and two finished, well off the pace.

Compressing vast amounts of hard work and heroism and a *soupcon* of lucky guessing, the team became competitive, but no more than that. This was a glorious era. Those who believe we've just now invented the modern engine would benefit from a look back at those days. Overhead camshafts, multiple-valve heads, exotic materials, effective suspensions, and a host of such technology as graces racing today were in place before World War I.

The racing was different and yet similar at the same time. Sports enthusiasts were still competing, but the big leagues were for the pros, on banked wooden speedways, board tracks as they were known, or full-mile ovals of packed dirt, horse tracks yanked into the industrial age. And there were professional hillclimbs, the easiest way to get up a contest. This was a time when politicians and preachers went on for hours so the public had no trouble, indeed may have insisted on, races of 200 or 300 mile duration on the mile tracks. The guys didn't get rich, but they did make more money and meet more girls than if they'd stayed on the farm or in the store.

There was a good crop of strong motorcycle makers at the time. Indian, Excelsior, Emblem, Merkel, and the amazing Cyclone, which never made a dime or did much on the road, but which had overhead camshafts while the others still had their valves next to the pistons.

Perhaps the most common link between then and now is that then, as now, power cost money. The team bikes needed more power, but not even Harley-Davidson was willing to spend it for a completely different engine.

Instead, in 1916, Harley introduced what we'd call a production-based racing engine.

The eight-valve racer in its element, the mile dirt track. Owner: Pete Smiley, Homeland, California.

Eccentric sprocket between primary and final drive chains lets chain tension be adjusted despite having engine and rear wheel rigid in the frame.

Before we get into its history, let the record show that the record *doesn't* show first, exactly what H-D did, second, just how they did it, and third, how many times it was done.

Begin with the basic components. By the scant evidence available today, the racing engineers used parts from the factory, such as engine cases and flywheels and other basics. They used the parts from the road-going F engine, an IOE design, and they kept with the F's bore and stroke of 3⁵/₁₆x3¹/₂in, for a displacement of 61ci, by no coincidence the limit for the major races.

The major engine change was of course the cylinder heads, which had two exhaust and two intake valves for each cylinder. The valves operated by a single camshaft in the timing case next

Linkage on front of frame tube lifts the exhaust valves off their seats when the rider pulls up. With high gearing and direct drive, the only way the engine could be started is with valves lifted and the machine towed fast enough for the valves to be dropped and compression restored.

to the flywheels, and via pushrods and rocker arms.

The theoretical advantage is easy to understand: The better an engine breathes, the more power it has. Four valves provide better breathing. Even more basic, having the valves above the pistons, with a direct route for the incoming and outgoing charges, is better than having the valves next to the piston or off to one side, as in the side-valve and IOE systems.

Full advantage couldn't be taken, however, mostly because the engineers of the day hadn't worked out the rules for octane requirements and combustion chamber shapes. But Harley-Davidson had the services of Harry Ricardo, an English engineer who was the world's leading expert on combustion chamber shape and intake flow, and the new engine clearly had the legs on the competition.

The engine had one carburetor, in the center of the vee, just like the road machines. (Yup, two would have been better. One tuner, England's Freddy Dixon, did such a conversion and it worked, but for the team, one was enough.)

Stock ignition was Bosch magneto. Lubrication was total loss, as in the F and J and the singles, but with both hand and automatic pumps. The breather tube from the crankcase was routed to aim at the primary chain. And notice the shiny clamp around the base of our example's front cylinder. That's an oiler. The direction of the flywheel's rotation and the direction of the machine's travel conspired to splash more oil up the back barrel than the front one. So they used internal baffles for the back and extra feed for the front.

There were three versions of the eight-valve engine, with different rocker arms and such, and with either the one-shaft, four-lobe camshaft or with two two-lobe cams, as in the example here. The first engines had short exhaust pipes, and the later ones—the bike pictured is in 1921 trim—had open ports.

Within that span, no two of the engines seem to have been alike. This wasn't done on purpose exactly; it was more a case of using the parts on hand, and tailoring the bike for the race it would be in. Photos exist of one eight-valve equipped with a bicycle pedal and crank starter, not seen on any of the other racers.

What the factory team, overseen by William S. Harley and directed by William Ottoway (who'd been lured away from Thor when H-D

began racing), had done was invent the racing stock engine. The eight-valve was more like, say, a NASCAR (National Association for Stock Car Automobile Racing) Chevy V-8, in that it looked sort of like the production version and began with the same parts, than an Ilmor Chevy engine, which comes from elsewhere with the sponsor's name and Bow Tie on it.

The stock-block engine went into a purely racing frame. It was called a keystone frame because although the overall view was a diamond bisected into fore and aft triangles, the front and center downtubes didn't meet. Instead there was a gap, joined by plates that carried the engine cases. Some of the bolts went right through, from plate to plate through the crankcases and thus held the engine together as well as fixing it in the frame and making the engine part of the structure. It was stiffer and because there was no frame tube below the cases, the engine sat lower. The rear wheel was fixed in the frame and the forks used Harley's leading links, which worked just fine on the track.

Now for the part about no two engines being alike. The basic eight-valve, listed in the catalog with year number and an R designation for racing, as in 16R or 17R, was described in the vaguest possible terms. The basic model would seem to have come with hardly anything at all: no clutch, no gearbox, no starter, never mind lights or other road equipment. The mile and board-track bikes didn't use brakes, on the grounds that being able to stop too quickly was risky for the chap behind. (No, I didn't make that up. As we'll see, brakes weren't allowed for another fifty years and in fairness it was much safer than you'd think.)

The basic eight-valve has only a compression release for starting, meaning you tow the bike, locked in gear with valves lifted off their seats, until there's some speed. When you drop the lever, compression returns and the engine fires, and you let go of the tow rope.

It also has a primary chain to the central sprocket. There's a second chain from the central sprocket, which in effect is filling in for a gearbox, to the rear sprocket. Look carefully at the central sprocket. The middle of the assembly is eccentric, so you can adjust the distance from there to the engine and thus adjust chain tension. They thought things out back then.

Beyond that, some of the eight-valves were made with sort of a slipper clutch in the rear hub.

44

Engine plates hold the crankcases and bridge the front and rear frame tubes; a Keystone frame, they said then. The lower end of this engine began life as the sporting version of the road-going IOE V-twin.

Riding was done in a full crouch, hands firm on the vertical grips, chin on the tank. The handle to the left of the twin caps—gas and oil—is the oil pump.

Next page
Two exhaust valves fed one massive and short exhaust port and stack: These engines literally breathed flames sometimes. The valve gear is external for better cooling and lubrication is by grease fittings on the rocker shafts.

46

There was a ring fixed to the axle and another ring on the rear sprocket, with spring-loaded dowels and holes. If the engine was shut off quickly, the force against the springs, caused by the rings trying to slide against each other, overcame the springs and the wheel and engine were disconnected, just for a second or two and just enough so the force didn't damage the drivetrain.

The factory brochure says clutch and brake, rear only at the time, were optional. They would have been needed, along with a gearbox, for road races.

Along the same lines, there were races and there were marathons. No specification was set for the fuel tanks, except that the one here looks bigger than normal, and was probably supplied for all-day races on the miles.

Priced *Not* To Sell

The lack of facts brings up the next point. In the ad, which didn't tell the prospective buyer much about the eight-valve racer, the prices are listed firmly at $1,500 F.O.B. Milwaukee for the eight-valve, $1,400 for the four-valve racer, which was the same machine but with only the front

cylinder fitted to the cases and eligible for the professional class on the smaller tracks. Indian meanwhile priced its eight-valve racer at $350, and the four-valve at $300.

Surely this can only have meant that the Harley-Davidson factory didn't want anybody to buy one of the racers and the Indian factory did. There are schools of thought that say what you get is what you wanted, so it's logical that in this case, Indian sold racing machines to the public, well, the professional racing public, and Harley didn't sell any. Not one.

The record is so vague here that all we can glean is that at least six eight-valves were built and there may have been as many as ten, with eight the middle estimate. Not even Steve Wright, the racing historian who's spent years on research and even built a dazzling replica of the eight-valve heads, or Willie G. Davidson, who now owns the machine Wright restored, knows for sure.

Instead, the team built machines for the team. By happy chance, Harley-Davidson was a power in the motorcycle business worldwide, with dealers and distributors everywhere there were roads and fuel. There was racing worldwide too, and the more influential dealers prevailed upon the home office to ship over some—we don't know how many in this case, either—of the eight-valves for their local stars to use.

The Records

Next on the list of what's been lost to history is just exactly how fast were the eight-valves? Better change *fast* to *powerful*. On February 22, 1921, at the one-mile board track at Fresno, California, Harley teamster Otto Walker topped time trials with a clocking of 107.78mph for a flying lap, and won the fifty-mile main event at an average of 101.43mph. It was the first motorcycle race in the world to be won at a speed of more than 100mph. Walker later averaged 104.43 in a twenty-five-mile race on the board track in Beverly Hills, California.

It would take more than sixty years for mile races to be won at those velocities again. Verdict is, the eight-valves were fast. How powerful we don't know, and we'd be foolish to guess.

Undercutting some of this was the fact that the other makes and even the other types were also fast. There was some strategy at work here. The accounts of the day hint that the team would send the eight-valves to the front, to wear the other chaps out, while the IOE Harleys were held in reserve: Obviously, if you use the same basic structure for two engines and one is more powerful than the other, the powerful engine will wear faster and break down sooner than the mild engine. Even so, the rivals in camp and out were not all that far behind.

The Harley Team was way out front. In 1921, they won all the national championship races. Every blessed one, easily justifying the "Wrecking Crew" nickname the newspapers had attached to the team.

So just before the start of the 1922 season, Harley-Davidson disbanded the team, quit winners as they say. Why? Historian Jerry Hatfield says his research indicates that enthusiasm for racing had waned, at the boardroom level anyway, and that winning and selling didn't seem as closely linked as they'd thought. According to Hatfield, Walter Davidson, in particular, was ticked off because Harley won Dodge City four times straight, yet the Dodge City police department kept on buying Indians.

That's foolish enough to be true. In any event, the team was dismissed. The riders and tuners became privateers. They went back to

Fitting at base of front cylinder is an oiler, provided because engine speed and direction of rotation splashed more oil to the rear barrel than to the front. Pipe from oiler to chain delivers oil mist at speed.

racing with and against each other on souped-up IOE engines, as they had before the factory fielded a team.

Restoration Impossible

The team's eight-valve machines were never seen again.

This is the sort of history one can't invent. Remember, the machines were deliberately priced so they wouldn't sell and there's no record of an eight-valve ever leaving the racing shop for private hands.

We can surmise that the riders were allowed to keep, more likely buy, the IOE engines because they were seen in action during the rest of the decade. The eight-valves were never seen in the United States again, however. The guys who know, Hatfield, Wright, John Cameron, and Pete Smiley, guess that the most likely reason is that they were junked.

Shock! Horror! Don't forget, nostalgia is a lot better than it used to be. Back in 1922 nobody cared about racing history, they just wanted to be racing's future. So there was no use for the engines in the shop, and outside they'd only be an embarrassment. If they won, they'd make the factory look bad, if they blew up, ditto. Smiley has even seen some bashed eight-valve parts.

You may be musing, at this juncture, if none of the eight-valves escaped from the team and there were only six, eight, or ten in the first place, how'd you get these new photos of what's obviously the real thing?

The survivors came home, from England and the Antipodes, which is a fancy way of saying Australia and New Zealand.

One can perhaps argue use of the plural here, though. If we're gonna be fussy, there's one and several fractions of an eight-valve left in the world, assembled into more machines than there are complete sets of parts.

The most complete survivor lives, of all places, in Italy. It's an especially odd example because it has clutch and three-speed gearbox and a loop frame, indicating that the Italian connection wanted a sporting road bike and used Harley-Davidson's top engine, the eight-valve, to power it.

The US examples are a varied lot. Willy G. owns an eight-valve built by Steve Wright, who spent countless hours and the sort of money that makes one hide the receipts from one's wife. Wright's engine and frame and cycle parts were

as built in the first place but because there were no eight-valve heads to be found, Wright commissioned a new set of patterns and castings.

John Cameron's eight-valve, now owned by Daniel Statnekov, of Tesuque, New Mexico, was brought back from England, where it was raced by Freddy Dixon. Because Cameron wanted to run the bike in the Bonneville speed trials, he parked the original cases and used the lower end from a two-cam road engine. Further, when the machine came home it was fitted with a stretched frame, to accommodate a clutch.

Current owner Statnekov is carefully rebuilding the race-version lower end and he still has hopes of finding an original short-coupled frame, which would give him the closest version of the real thing.

Meanwhile, the bike pictured is as close to the true example as anybody has come since the eight-valves disappeared.

Owner Pete Smiley turned up an engine in New Zealand. "It was a shell, no flywheels or other internals and I didn't even know the man had the frame," says Smiley.

But he did, albeit the frame was bent out of shape. That was no problem for Smiley, who ran his own speedway team and did special projects for factory NASCAR and Indy teams. Plus, because he'd already been restoring race bikes and was plugged into the network, Smiley rustled up the tanks and other cycle parts. There were lugs on the forks for a friction damper, which didn't come on the frame but which he'd seen in race photos, so he made a damper of his own.

Perhaps the oddest detail here is the tires. They are original racing tires from the board-track era, just as they were found and presumably were raced. "Firestones last," says Smiley. "I've never seen a surviving Goodyear from that era."

The actual engine represents what could have been done by a private owner of that time. The heads are so authentic they were used to make the patterns for Wright's reproductions, while the cases are two-cam F, the road-going 61ci of 1921. Except that way back then the factory had special engines with optimum balance and maximum clearances. They were coded with numbers that began with 500. What Smiley has here, eight-valve heads atop cases marked 21FH523, is what could have been raced in 1921.

They were brave men in those days.

With machines to match.

The major engine change was of course the cylinder heads, which had two exhaust and two intake valves for each cylinder. Four valves provided the engine with better breathing.

Chapter 5

WJ Sport Twin

Something Completely Different

No Harley-Davidson has ever been less like the rest of the family than the WJ Sport Twin.

Nor has any miscalculation ever come from better motives. During World War I, H-D was busy with the war effort, supplying thousands of sturdy V-twins to the armed services. Back home, much thought was given to what the world would want when peace returned.

Harley-Davidson's management decided there would be a need for what one could call a gentleman's motorcycle: clean, quiet, low-stress, practical transportation. So the engineering department designed a very different twin-cylinder engine and cycle parts to fit.

The engine was an opposed twin, a boxer, with a central crankshaft and a throw for each cylinder so the pistons went in and out at the same time. The forces generated nearly cancel each other, so this was a much smoother engine than a V-twin could hope to be. The W engine, as the factory designated it, used a very small crankcase with the flywheel outside the cases but encased in sheet metal. Bore and stroke were 2.75x3.00in, about 36ci or 600cc (cubic centimeters), and claimed power was a modest 6bhp.

The cylinder heads were cast integrally with the cylinders, which took care of the gasket problem. There were screw-in caps outboard (one can't say "above" with the cylinders horizontal) of the valves, which were in the cylinders, so the owner could easily remove and service the valves and the replaceable valve seats. By alternating the firing order, with the front piston on compression and the rear one on the exhaust stroke, power pulses were evenly delivered *and* a central set of cam lobes could open both sets of valves.

There was one carburetor, at the right rear of the machine. The carb fed a rather long intake manifold. But the runners for the intake were perched atop the centralized exhaust manifold, so the length of the intake tract was heated by the exhaust, with the heat making up for the loss of atomization the long intake pipes would otherwise suffer.

The Sport Twin is a machine that lends itself to being walked around, slowly and carefully.

The kick lever, or step-start, as they called it and really a better way to describe what one does with it, is on the left side of the machine, unlike the other Harleys or rival Indians. The factory's engineering records don't mention this, so we can only guess that the layout of the power takeoff, the clutch, and the three-speed gearbox forced the location, or perhaps it's because the carb had to go where the step-start would have otherwise been.

Sport Twin was a Harley-Davidson for the gentleman rider, of whom alas there were fewer than the makers hoped. Owner: Armando Magri, Sacramento, California.

The only brake was in the rear hub. As this arm implies, the brake was coaster style, as used on bicycles.

Next page
This is a different Harley. Rocking link forks aren't like anything The Motor Company used before, during or since the Sport's time. The enclosed chain is ahead of its time and the step-start is on the left because that's where there was room for it.

Tanks for oil and gas were slung beneath the top frame rail, with oil pump integral with the tank and gearshift gate attached on the left.

If the guy on the Indian Scout passed the Sport Twin owner on the hill or highway, it didn't make the WJ owner feel any better to not have to oil his chain.

The engine and gearbox were one unit, with the gears above the crankcase. The engine sat very low in the machine, which also lowered the center of gravity. The engine and transmission bridged the frame tubes, a design known then as the keystone frame, and the complete machine weighed only 265lb, a factory claim later checked and verified on certified scales. There was an automatic oiling system to supplement the traditional pump and yes, the final drive is by enclosed chain, speaking of ideas well ahead of their time. And the crankcase breather delivered its oil mist to the chain in the cover, taking care of that maintenance bother.

The rear brake was a contracted shoe that wrapped around the drum and was tightened by a foot lever. The model shown has no front brake, but a similar unit was also an option for the front wheel late in the model's production. Oh, and the W model came with magneto and the WJ with battery-powered ignition and Harley's own lighting system.

The front suspension deserves extra attention. It's a link, like the other contemporary Harley-Davidson design, but where the others are leading link, this one has its pivot in the center, sort of a rocking trailing link. The fender moves with the frame rather than the wheel, and above the fender and sharing the bracket is another rocker. When the front of that rocker is pulled down by the action of the links, the single, central spring is compressed.

The Sport Twin was different. One could fairly say that some features, the enclosed chain for example, were clearly an improvement, while the front suspension was probably as good as but no better than Harley's original.

The Sport Twin got off to an advantageous start. By 1918 Harley-Davidson was the largest motorcycle manufacturer in the world. Even while supplying most of the war's motorcycles, H-D had the capacity to do more, so when the war ended the company was able to supply accumulated demand while second-place Indian was still busy with the military. Early in the run, the Sport Twin was the most popular solo machine on the market.

Nor did the distinctive bike lack achievement. A WJ was the first motorcycle to climb Mount Baldy, the Los Angeles landmark. Another Sport Twin set a record for the Three Flags Run, from Canada to Mexico, beating the pre-

Long thin engine gave room for floorboards but required what has to be one of the longest intake manifolds—from carburetor at central left—ever designed.

vious record holder, a 61ci machine, by better than five hours. Next came a new record for Chicago to Denver, this time bettering a four-cylinder motorcycle. And when one of the day's best-known explorers toured Death Valley, he did it on a Sport Twin, and said so. The company wasn't exactly unwilling to publicize all this, either. At a time when roads were dirt and maps figments of the imagination, such travel meant adventure and having a bike that could handle the task was vital.

The Sport Twin was also the mainstay of Harley-Davidson's vigorous export business. The Europeans loved the idea behind the model, and the way it worked.

So why then did production of the Sport Twin stop in 1923? The market demand didn't justify the model's existence. And the reason for that is . . .

. . . Competition. Indian returned in force with the Sport Scout, a V-twin with more power than the Sport Twin could muster, and with a raucous edge to that performance. On the other end of the spectrum, by 1920 Henry Ford had the price of a Model T down to $395, against the Sport Twin's $380.

People are odd. When we make fun of the big, clumsy cars that ruled our highways in the past, when we praise the little cars of the present and wonder why the car makers were so foolish for so long, we forget that all during the 1930s, 1940s, and 1950s, little cars came on the market, and failed. As Samuel Goldwyn is supposed to have said, if people don't want to go to the movies, you can't stop them.

By the same token, if the guy with the Scout passed the Sport Twin owner on the hill or the highway, it didn't make the WJ owner feel any better to not have to oil his chain.

And if the family could buy a car for the same money that it paid for a motorcycle without even a sidecar, guess who picked the car and who said,

The Sport Twin was the mainstay of Harley-Davidson's vigorous export business. The Europeans loved the idea behind the model, and the way it worked.

Previous page
The WJ stands alone as a different bike. The rocking, trailing link forks were unique to this truly unique bike. The fender moves with the frame instead of the wheel. Harley-Davidson had never done it before, and hasn't done it again since the WJ.

Sport's gearbox had three speeds forward, with shifting by left hand and the clutch a pedal for the left foot.

Headlight by now has become electric, with a bulb and power from a generator.

"Yes, Dear," in the firm, manly way we husbands have.

You could say the Sport Twin was ahead of its time, a concept that simply arrived too early to be appreciated.

Or you could listen to the old-timers, who wonder if by 1922 the sporting riders already had learned that the true sound of the real motorcycle was the asymmetric thunder of the V–twin.

Chapter 6

1926 JD

The Big Twin Comes of Age

This is a legend that began after its time. This is the story of the JD, whose time was 1926—in the case of the example pictured here—the model's second production year. Historically, its time began with the V–twin and the pocket-valve engine, IOE (intake over exhaust) and both set off to one side of the bore, as we've already seen. By the beginning of the First World War, the motorcycle was a viable mode of transportation. Technical progress is war's only useful product and there was lots of that, so as the 1920s began Harley-Davidson offered a line of small single-cylinder models for the practical rider: the intriguing fore-and-aft Sport Twin for those who didn't want what the other guys wanted, and the Model JD big twin for those who did.

Power, is what we've begun to see here. The original twin displaced 61ci, the classic 1000cc. In 1921 H-D took the easiest route to more power and increased the size of the bore, which took the displacement from 61 to 74ci, surely the most classic of Harley measurements.

But that model was mostly what we've already seen, a bit dated and not as modern in looks as were the rival twins from Indian, so in 1925, the JD got seriously updated.

The most important improvement was a new frame, which lowered the engine; one assumes this could be done because more roads were paved and those that weren't were smoother than the ruts of the wagon-trail days. The frame had stronger tubes, with the front and rear downtubes joined by a plate that also carried the engine, predicting the semi-stressed engines that we'd see sixty years later.

Then, as now, the height or lack of height of the seat was a selling and bragging point. On the new frame, the seat was a full 3in lower than on the earlier models. And the seat was sprung, with a sliding post that used the rear frame tube for guidance, atop a spring. The rear wheel was of course mounted solidly in the frame, but when you hit that huge pothole or slammed across the tracks or whatever, the floating seat cushioned the blow. (It also gave a stately sort of cadence to the ride on bad roads. It saved my spine many times on my old 74 and worked so well right up to the last of the real FLHs, I was sorry to see it go. In fact, I'm not sure you can really understand why the Harleys back then were such good all-day machines if you haven't ridden one with the floating seat post.)

Some practical changes were made to the JD, such as hinging the lower portion of the rear fender so you could extract the wheel when a tire went flat, which they did a lot back then.

The spindly look was out. The JD (and the 61ci J) used fatter—27x3½in from 28x3in—

Lower engine and larger tanks dictated generous cutouts in the tank sides and bottom for the valve gear. Owner: Johnny Eagles, Orange, California.

Next page
The JD's IOE engine displaced a full 74ci, and was that engine design's peak.

tires, measured from outside to outside. Balloon tires, we'd say now. And there were larger and rounder fuel tanks, which were nicknamed balloon tanks.

The JD's engine was more refined than radical. An oil pump driven off the gearcase was added to be sure the crankcase got a steady supply of lubricant. Not much, though. The system was still total loss, but now the supply didn't depend on the rider remembering to use the pump. And there was still a hand pump for the long hill or open stretch. Speaking of the open road, the JD's muffler was a built-in baffle, with a device that turned the baffle aside when you cleared the city limits.

The JD engine was (obviously) a refinement of the IOE V-twins seen already, with the intake valve above the exhaust valve and both set in the combustion chamber next to, rather than above, the cylinder bore. The 1926 JD shown here used *one* camshaft with four lobes, one for each valve, a system. Later in the J series, with the 1929 JD and JDH, there would be two shafts, side by side, each with two lobes, one for each cylinder. They were known as "two cam" motors, understandably enough, although the Harley singles of the time used two shafts with one lobe each and weren't known as two-cam motors. At any rate, when the IOE was replaced by the side-valve twins, the side-valve engines used a row of four one-lobe cams and the single stick with four lobes was reintroduced for the ohv (overhead valve) Model E of 1936. The big twin still uses one camshaft and the current XL, which you can't exactly call the little twin as it's now grown to a displacement of 74ci, same as the JD here, has the row of lobes. Harley-Davidson doesn't change things on the spur of the decade, even.

What H and D offered with the Model JD was mostly a good, stout, serviceable motorcycle. Perhaps not the Model T of motorcycles, however, because this was a larger and more expensive model than you'd get for basic transportation. But well up to the job.

The example pictured, owned by collector Johnny Eagles since 1959, began life as the private bike of a motor officer, was in daily use for its first decade, then sat in a collection and now is back on the road. Notice that the tires and rims have been modernized and that Eagles has added a front brake, which the JD didn't come with until 1928. "I like to ride on the street," is how Eagles explains the changes.

The motorcycle market declined in the late 1920s, presumably because Henry Ford was cutting prices on the Model T cars, so the JD did well enough, keeping Harley-Davidson ahead of Indian in sales.

But Indian had done some homework and was building side-valve engines that could run with the IOEs, while being cheaper and neater. Harley committed to the flathead route and in 1930 introduced a replacement line of 74s, side-valves each and every one.

(Pause for a moment here.) For some strange reason, Harley-Davidson has always had trouble with new models. So it was with the flatheads. In fact, they created so much difficulty that there was a massive recall campaign and even when the revised engine was on the market, the VL 74 was more than 100lb heavier than the JD, with about the same power.

Still, there are accounts of the better dealers making the new machines good and then luring the owners of the older bikes into going for long rides, during which the Js collapsed and the VLs kept running.

In spite of that, because the JDs kept running during a time of economic hardship—we're

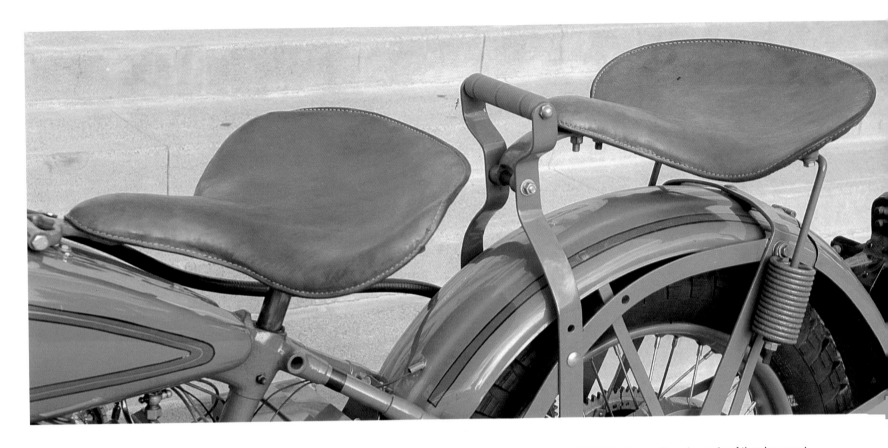

Rough roads of the day must have required something other than the operator for the passenger to hang on to. The operator meanwhile got a seat that slid on its post.

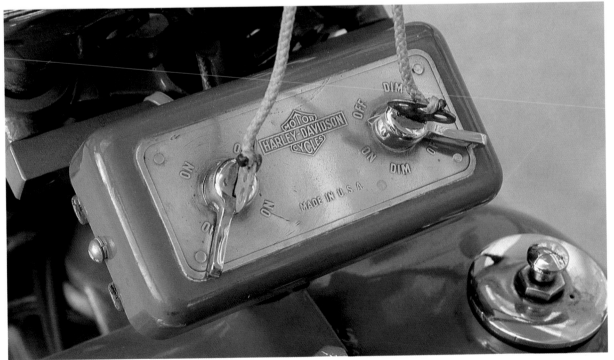

Control box has the ignition switch on the left, light switch on the right.

Options of the day included a passenger seat. Options added since, the front brake for instance and the rear view mirrors, are there because the owner uses his machine in modern traffic and for long trips.

into the 1930s here—a legend began that the JD was always better than the newer engines, in every way, kind of like the way your dad still talks about the Duesenberg or Joe Louis.

You could say it was only nostalgia and the glow of youth at work.

Except that when the American Motorcyclist Association (AMA) set up new racing rules for the 1930s, there was a semi-pro class, Class B, for hillclimbs and TTs and the rules allowed 61s

with overhead-valves, or pocket-valves, or 80ci flatheads.

The JD engines ruled the roost until the AMA came to the defense of the newer machines and presumably the factories, by banning the pocket-valves. That was in 1939, ten years after production stopped.

So there had to be something behind the legend, after all.

Passenger seat gets springs and the stoplight delivers a message for those who need extra help.

Among the practical changes on the JD was the hinged lower portion of the rear fender so you could extract the wheel when a tire went flat, which they did a lot back then.

65

Chapter 7

1936 VLH

The Best of the Side-valve Vs

Red is the word here. After all those years of grey and olive drab, Harley-Davidson discovered colors, as in the bright red used for the VLH in 1936. Owner: Frank Gorzny, Idlewild, California.

Remember the Zen question about the big tree, how if it fell in the woods and there wasn't anybody to hear it, would there be a noise?

This is a story like that. Except that it's a Harley-Davidson story, so we'll begin way back in 1930, when the IOE J series was replaced with the side-valve V series, still displacing 74ci but with a better frame and more modern design. Everything was fine on paper, but in H-D tradition the first year was a disaster. The design was basically sound while some of the parts, as in the flywheels, were small and weak. So many problems occurred right after the introduction that many Harley fans and owners kept their JDs and to this day claim that the older design was a better one.

Actually, the V and later VL, L meaning higher compression albeit nobody remembers why, were good, sound, big bikes. The VL was at least a match for the big Indians, which was all that mattered because the other makes had folded and the foreigners were busy watching their own markets collapse.

Racing in the early 1930s was pretty much as it had been when we saw the eight-valve retire, with specialized machines built to a precise formula. And taxes were based on retail value, while in other countries you paid for the size of the engine.

This leads to what could be called the aircraft principle, that is, getting a level of performance (in this case, displacement) the most efficient way possible, as opposed to the European system, which was based on racing and/or tax avoidance, of leaning on the engine to get more power from the same displacement.

Times were tough when Harley-Davidson began working on a really new engine, the ohv 61 that would appear in 1936. It was supposed to appear earlier but there were teething troubles and economic worries. What it came down to is sort of a factory hot rod, perhaps the first of such.

Late in 1935 a new, make that improved, side-valve model appeared. It was called the VLH. It appeared in the showrooms by the handful. It never appeared in the catalog or the sales brochures, however, and I can think of a couple of H-D histories that left it out too.

The VLH's official debut came in model year 1936, which means late 1935, when the sales push began according to tradition.

The engineers simply took the normal VL, the 74 with the higher of the two compression ratios offered, and moved the crankpin outboard between the flywheels, so the stroke was 4.25in rather than 4in. Same bore, 3.42in (or 3$^{7}/_{16}$in if you prefer fractions, which the factory's material doesn't always state). The result of this simple

The control box now also holds an ammeter, to report on the condition of the charging system and battery. This example's owner has added accessories from back then, a pair of dice that came up seven.

H-D noted the paints and colors on the market and in 1933 the drab olives were replaced with reds and blacks on regular order, as opposed to owners having to know the secret code for special orders.

change was a displacement of 80ci, and a gain of 10 percent or so of horsepower.

Everything else remained the same, such as the frame and suspension, wheels and tires, tanks and so forth. The engine used the total loss oiling system, which would be replaced with a dry sump design on the Model E.

One more useful item added was a gearbox with four speeds forward. This was an option, and an obscure option. The four speeds were used in the same space as the older three forward and one reverse used for the sidecar models, and the VLH's gears went inside the same case as used for the Model 61. But the actual gears and shafts and related parts aren't the same at all.

Why did they do it? Not even Jerry Hatfield's detailed search of the directors' notes turns up anything definite. We can surmise a few facts, though.

Times were tough and the fighting got rough. Indian and Harley-Davidson were the surviving motorcycle makers. Actually, Indian was acting stronger and moving faster than H-D

was. It introduced its dry-sump oil system in 1933, after the H-D design work began, but before the Harley engine was ready for the market.

Indian had an 80-incher on the market, a really big twin.

And Indian had been bought by one of the DuPonts—yup, *the* DuPonts—and the connection had given the company access to the best and brightest paints. H-D took note and in 1933 the drab olives were replaced with reds and blacks on regular order, as opposed to knowing the secret code for special orders.

Notes from management meetings during the early 1930s show a predictable mix of hope and fear: Bold steps were taken, as in the approval of the ohv engine project, and on at least one occasion the founders wondered if they shouldn't simply close down the firm, as Excelsior's owners had done.

The balance between these two extremes was to keep working on the Model 61, delay its introduction when things didn't go as planned,

Gear lever and speedometer mounted atop the twin tanks.

and—this is a surmise—to deliver a low-cost ace in the hole.

The VLH was just that. If performance would help sell bikes, and it always has, then performance would be improved. A modern and efficient engine was the best way to go, but a larger version of the older engine was the easiest hedge.

That's what they did. We can further surmise that the hedge arrived just in time for management to be sure the ohv engine would actually work, and get there only a little late, so the big flathead quietly went into production. At that time, the extra performance of the old engine might have drawn attention away from the new engine.

All of which makes sense, and all of which worked to obscure what Bud Ekins, an expert on the era, says was the best of the side-valve big twins.

Factory hot rods are usually fun and practical, as in the Buick Century or Plymouth Road Runner of later eras. They work because the enthusiasts who run them know how far to go, as opposed to those of us who improve our machines right out of the ballpark.

In the case of the 1936 VLH (not a bad play on words, eh?), the basic gain was that the 80-incher was an honest 100mph motorcycle. This was very important. Hard to imagine now, but at one time the world wanted to run faster and better. The 1930s were a time of speed records set on land, sea, and air on almost a daily basis. Riders like Dot Robinson, by the books the best woman motorcyclist ever, and Fred Ham were making coast-to-coast runs and 1,000-mile rides. The ordinary bike nut could—and did—go out on the highway and open 'er up, and the enthusiast with a machine that would hit that magic century could collect a lot of root beer on the strength of the claim.

Next, the '36 was light for its power, meaning it would handle well and corner at speed and take the jumps and ruts that were part of life at the time: Not by accident have Harleys always been at home on graded dirt and gravel roads.

The 1936 VLH was the side-valve big twin's day in the sun. Even if its design was obsolete by then, it's possible to wish that its day had been a bit longer and that the sun had shone more brightly.

Fishtail muffler was based on a racing design supposed to reduce noise without, well, muffling the flow of exhaust. The tubing outboard of the regular frame—called crash bars until the lawyers got involved; called case guards since—was a popular option of the time.

Speaking of extra, sixty years ago Harley folks were as ready to proclaim their loyalty as they are now, and The Motor Company catered to this with a full line of caps and jackets.

Third, nothing was really new about the machine itself. Move the crankpin out and reinforce a few bits, that was all it took. The traditional teething troubles were absent for this one, so the few who knew about the 80 simply rode the thing home. (As we'll see next, the many who knew about the Model 61 didn't have it quite so easy.)

Then came progress. The ohv 61 was a better machine, nostalgia to the contrary. Good breathing is even more efficient than more displacement. And while the factory improved the Knucklehead (detailed in the next chapter) by making it stronger, the VLH was improved by putting the 80ci side-valve engine into a larger frame, same as the one for the 61, and by giving the side-valver the dry sump, recirculating oil system seen on the 61 and on rival Indians.

By engineering standards, these were improvements. But the ohv engine could take advantage of the added strength, and the side-valve was saddled by added weight. The 1937 VHL was slower than the Model E, and heavier

and slower than the first 80. The side-valve engine was kept in the model line-up as the UH, the letter change meaning the larger engine *and* the newer frame, until the 61 was treated to a larger stroke and became the F, of classic 74ci.

The 1936 VLH was the side-valve Big Twin's day in the sun. The design was obsolete by then but even so, it's possible to wish that the day had been a bit longer and that the sun had shone more brightly.

The VL was top of the line, a road machine with full fenders and lights. The VLH was nearly a secret, with the extra displacement and power carried by a frame and running gear nearly unchanged from the 74ci version.

Chapter 8

1936 Model E

Why the Legend Lives

This is the Knucklehead, the best and boldest move in Harley-Davidson history.

This is a second generation of courage.

One could argue that the introduction in 1936 of the overhead-valve Model E, a 61ci V-twin, was a display of more faith and determination than shown when the company was founded. After all, when that happened times were good, people were crazy about motorbikes, and the founders had the support of families, friends, and suppliers.

But in 1936 the United States and the world were still slumping into the trough of the Great Depression. Motorcycle sales were reckoned in four figures and the best way to illustrate the position of the owners is to say that when they cut the pay of salaried employees by 10 percent, they cut their own salaries in half. Things were so bad the directors debated whether to stay in business or close down and keep their savings intact.

But back in 1931, when the stock market crash of 1929, the Dust Bowl, the bank failures, and the tariff wars were still hoped to be mere stutters on the way back to prosperity, the board had authorized a new model. Really new.

Nor did the improvements come too soon. Early Harleys were thoroughly contemporary and some, the eight-valve racer for instance or the Sport Twin, may have been ahead of their time. But by the late 1920s the edge was off and the name Harley-Davidson meant reliable, quiet, side-valve engines in sturdy workday form.

So William S. Harley, the founding engineer, knew what he was doing when he proposed a new engine design.

There would be two major changes. The first involved the lubrication system. Until that time, most motorcycles had used what's called total loss oiling. The term misleads. The oil isn't lost. Instead, there's a supply of oil in a separate tank. A pump, hand or mechanical, delivers oil to the crankcase. Only a few ounces are needed to keep the metal surfaces cool and slick and the pump supplies fresh oil at the same rate it's used, whether burned or leaked away. Not a bad system when engines run slowly and the pump (or the rider) gets the delivery rate right. But that didn't always happen, so Harley proposed a more modern system, with an engine-driven pump that sent oil to the engine and brought it back to the tank, making sure the engine always had just enough.

Second, side-valves are cheap and quiet and nearly maintenance free. But if you imagine the valves parallel with and next to the cylinder, you'll see that the air-fuel mixture takes a twisted path in and out. And, to make room for

The Model E was a daring move for 1936, as sleek and modern as, say, a diesel locomotive styled in the same era. Owner: Armando Magri, Sacramento, California.

Real headlight and compact horn were the new order. The plate outboard of the fork springs and the knob below the plate are a friction damper to tune the front suspension.

The rocker shafts are held in place by nuts which are positioned in the castings just so, making the top of the engine look like the back of a fist, with the nuts being knuckles. Thus, the engine became known as the Knucklehead.

the valves to open you need space above them, next to the cylinder. That's where the combustion takes place and where the heated mixture expands. Your motive force has to move sideways and the combustion chamber's shape is a compromise. Side-valve engines have been cajoled and

coerced into miracles of power and performance. But plainly put, they aren't as good as engines with valves overhead, in the cylinder head and directly opposite the cylinder. Harley wanted to make a production engine with ohv, a first for H-D despite years of making race engines in that

Four speeds forward now, but still shifted by hand and with a rocker pedal to control the clutch with the left foot.

form and with the intake valve overhead and the exhaust valve below it, as on the earlier road engines.

In 1931 they planned to produce the new model for the 1935 model year. Then things got rough. The engineering staff was reduced in size and the prototype engines weren't right and wouldn't you know it, Indian went to the new system, dry sump as they called it, in 1933. As late as June 1935, the prospects for the new model were so gloomy that the notes from the directors' meeting say, "We will probably go ahead with the job."

They did. Early deliveries were slow, mostly so changes could be made before things went too far, but perhaps also to use dealers and customers as an involuntary test fleet.

Never mind that. The new machine followed Harley practice of using a letter, E in this case, to designate the engine. The plain E was the low-compression model, 6.5:1 with a claimed 37bhp, and there was the optional EL (why H-D uses L for higher compression no one has ever explained) with 7:1 compression ratio and 40bhp. Bore and stroke were 3⁵⁄₁₆x3¹⁄₂in, for 61ci. That's a classic displacement for Harleys (or Indians or a host of European engines, where it's 1000cc), and the E was quickly known as the Sixty-One.

Just as quickly came the bike's better nickname. The right sides of the cylinder heads are topped by castings that receive the pushrods and their covers and carry the rocker arms. The rocker shafts are held in place by nuts which are positioned in the castings just so, making the top of the engine look like the back of a fist, with the nuts being knuckles. Thus the engine became known as the Knucklehead, creating a tradition that's with us still.

With the new engine came a new frame (actually it was designed for the big side-valve twins as well), an improved version of the springer front end, new tanks and instrument panel, and a new gearbox with four forward speeds and a better way to shift them. Technical historian Jerry Hatfield points out that we don't actually shift gears anymore. The gears are in constant mesh. What we shift are the things that connect or disconnect the gears to their shafts and each other.

Visually, the 61 E was a masterpiece. There's a saying in design that what *looks* right, *is* right. The 61 E looked perfect: clean, compact, and packed with mechanical functions. The engine filled the frame's vee; the oil tank firmed the gap between rear hub and engine. It was absolutely right.

There were problems at first, though; in fact, the oiling system was more complicated than they'd expected and there were leaks and gaps and the frame wasn't strong enough to handle the power. At least 100 running changes were made between the first and last of the 1936 Model Es.

At the same time, they had planned to build 1,600 and the sales totaled at least 1,945. Not to gloat, but in the same year as Harley's bold and daring move in the right direction, Indian brought out a new in-line four, which proved to be a weak machine and the worst thing they could have done.

Taking it one step further, for the generation preceding the Model E, Harley-Davidson was best in quality control and production skill, while Indian had the nod in technical advances and design. The Knucklehead took that away. It was good from the start and as flaws surfaced, they were taken care of. Harley-Davidson took the technical lead in 1936 and Indian never got close again.

The final part of the story is too good to be fiction. The Model 61 became the 74 and they changed the heads and then the lower end and the heads again and the crankcase again, and so it went.

In fact, it's still going on. Obviously the 1992 F engine, the blockhead, the 80, the Evolution engine, call it what you wish, is different in every

Previous page
Box at lower right holds tools and parts, small chromed brackets on the sides of the fender are to tie down luggage.

The 61 was more sporting than the larger side-valve 74, more powerful than the smaller 45, and aimed at the true enthusiast—who else would buy in the depth of a depression?—or police departments needing an answer to the Ford V-8.

There's one camshaft with four lobes at the center of the vee formed by the pushrod tubes. The ignition timer, in Harley's terms, is to the left of the vee and is driven by gears in the timing case.

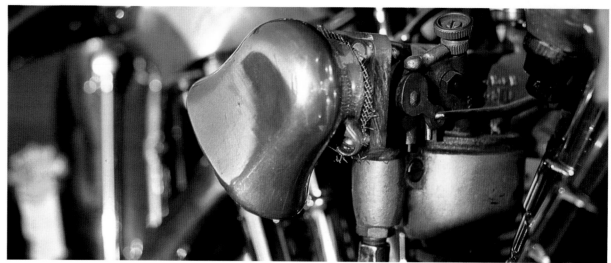

The air intake is bell-shaped and fronts the carburetor feeding the new engine.

detail from this 1936 Knucklehead. But in concept, the 1992 is the same overall design as the 1936. Talk about economic miracles, the engine that pulled Harley-Davidson through the Depression is still hauling away. Surely this is the longest-lived engine design ever.

Not only that, but there are people in other places—wink nudge—who are copying this design and they still can't capture the spirit.

Sometimes what goes around, keeps right on going.

The entire machine was virtually all new, as in frame, engine, gearbox, fuel tank, and fenders. The oil tank for the dry sump system is aft of the engine and below the seat.

Chapter 9

1948 Model S

Too Little, Too Early

Failure is an orphan, as the Chinese proverb puts it. No H-D executive ever stepped forward to point that out back in 1947, about the time Soichiro Honda was bolting industrial engines to surplus bicycles, Harley-Davidson introduced a radical new type of motorcycle to the youth of America.

They won't brag about this bike for the plainest of reasons: The youth of America turned up its collective nose at it, or Mom and Pop turned down their thumbs, or maybe the idea of a tiny Harley-Davidson was a fine idea at the worst time.

Whichever, the story of the Model S isn't a success story. More like a fable complete with moral, which is that having a good idea isn't always enough.

The fable begins with H-D's survival of the Depression and its revival during World War II. Just about every factory in the United States hummed busily during the war, which cured the Depression. Harley turned out military motorcycles among other things. The military doesn't like innovation, and the engineering and sales departments had lots of time to consider what to do when the war ended. Hard times had deprived people of fun, ditto for the war, except that the war put money into previously empty pockets. There was a tremendous pent-up demand for

goods and recreation, and the men at the top of The Motor Company knew it.

They also knew they needed to lower the floor, so to speak. All during the 1930s the founders worried because they didn't have machines small and cheap enough to lure the youth market, not that the term was in use yet.

The end of hostilities provided what seemed the perfect solution. The winners had decided that the losers owed piles of money for starting the war. A German motorcycle company, DKW, had been making a neat little two-stroke single. Harley-Davidson in the United States and BSA in England were given the rights to produce the DKW engine as a reward for their war work and punishment for DKW.

We need to digress here. Two-strokes, as all racing fans of the 1970s, 1980s, and 1990s know, are the most powerful and lightest way to win races, at the cost of ferocious complexity and temperament.

In 1947 this wasn't merely not so, it was backward. Two-strokes were industrial powerplants, woefully weak for their displacement and useful only because they had fewer parts than four-strokes did and thus cost less to make. They were small and light because they didn't crank out enough power to stress their components—easy to see why the executives and de-

Model S was tiny, with a wheelbase of 50in and a dry weight of 200lb. Owner: David Hansen, Ventura, California.

Headlight nacelle houses the speedometer and echoes the larger, home-built Harleys.

signers reckoned they could produce a motorcycle that would attract buyers away from bicycles and scooters and not detract from the appeal of the factory's twins.

The new model appeared late in 1947, as a 1948. It was called either the M-125 or the S-125, depending on which sales brochure you read.

(For added confusion, later versions carried the appealing name of Hummer, by which all the two-strokes came to be known, which ticks off the experts something fierce.)

The Model S was a different Harley. The engine was mostly DKW; bore and stroke of 2.06x 2.28in, for a displacement of 7.6ci or 125cc,

roughly. Output was about 3bhp and you had to mix the oil with the gas yourself—a different version of total loss oiling.

The frame was full loop, single tube. The rear wheel bolted solidly in place and the front suspension was girder, with legs that went up and down carrying the front hub and wheel. This wasn't at all like the springer forks of the larger Harleys. One is reminded here of the Sport Twin (see chapter 5), another example of what seemed to be a different design team working in the same plant. The S had tiny drum brakes, a solo seat, and a little fuel tank, which later was pirated by the racers, leading to a faddish racer

look. And that, kids, is why the current XLH has too small a fuel tank, but that's another story.

If there was a surprise from this design, it would be that the shift was controlled by the right foot and the clutch by the left hand. It made sense to the engineers because that's how DKW did it. But back then the real Harleys, the 74s, 61s, and 45s, still had hand shift and foot clutch, so the Model S did some pioneering for its larger and older siblings.

The S came with a strictly solo seat, rightfully so as the 125's 3bhp would push the machine and occupant to perhaps 55mph on a good day. The marketing staff must have had some say

This example is unrestored— as found, you could say—and judging from the missing front fender and oversized front tire, led a hard life.

Carried over from the DKW version was this little pointer: Forget which gear you're in? Look down and see to which number the arrow points.

The youth of America turned up its collective nose at the Model S, or Mom and Pop turned down their thumbs, or maybe the idea of a tiny Harley-Davidson was a fine idea at the worst time.

here because you could order a windshield and saddlebags just like those for the FLs and WLs. This was a time when Chevrolet buyers liked to order extras to replicate Cadillacs and Buicks, and you could get fake fuel tanks for your bicycle. It follows then that the same peer pressure was applied to motorcycles.

None of which made much of a difference with the Model S. The thing was new and people did want new machines, so sales began as a modest success. But that's all that happened. Summing up several frustrating decades, the tiddler got better suspension, a larger engine, and a keen name, to no avail. Then came singles from Italy, and later H-D's four-stroke engine was replaced by a two-stroke. Harley offered enduro models, set some records, and even had a motocross team, all to no avail as well. There simply wasn't enough demand for the singles, not when (to be brutally honest) you could get more motorcycle for the same or less price from you-know-where.

The Model S is included here because its commercial failure had nothing to do with the actual product. The Hummer, a term used defiantly because when I was a kid, hurumph, they were all called Hummers, worked fine *if you understood it.*

Armando Magri, retired owner of the best dealership I've ever been in, says there were two big problems with the tiddlers.

The first was sort of mechanical: In Europe even little bikes were for adults, who were

presumed to know how to take care of what was for them a major investment. Here, a 125 was a toy, to be left outside in the rain next to the wrenches Junior had taken from Dad's workbench. If you took care of the machines, Magri says, they'd take care of you. He even sponsored an owners club and they all had fun Humming through the woods.

The second obstacle had to do with psychology: Dealers and owners of *real* Harleys didn't like the singles or the people who rode in on them. No matter what the factory did, no matter how attractive the kids and women in the ads, if you walked into the dealership and wanted to talk two-stroke, you were ignored if you were lucky and derided if you weren't. So the newcomers and the kids went elsewhere and the motorcycle was reinvented by other chaps, and we all know what happened after that.

Which brings us to the punchline: The Model S was an ordinary motorcycle in itself. It was significant more as a symbol, an object lesson, and an illustration of, as Sherlock Holmes said of the Giant Rat of Sumatra, a story for which the world was not yet ready.

Engineering was pre-war, with rigid rear wheel and girder—not Harley's leading link—front suspension.

85

Chapter 10

WR

The Birth of Production Racing

If good racing is when you don't know who's going to win, then the lowest point in American motorcycle competition came in 1935, when one man won every, yes *every*, event on the national schedule.

If the bad news is that racing went down in flames, then the good news is that out of the ashes came the best racing the world has ever seen.

The vehicle through which motorcycle racing reached its high point was the Harley-Davidson WR.

Begin with the debacle. The culprit was the Great Depression. Racing during the 1920s and early 1930s was done with special engines and frames. They were exotic overhead valve and cam designs, made for racing only. They were powerful and expensive and as a rule only the factories could afford to run them. The only limit was displacement. Two professional classes existed: A for 21ci singles and 45ci twins, and B for 45 and 80ci twins or fours, which were too heavy to compete but were still eligible. When times were good there was money enough and factories enough for competition to be equal. But when sales slumped, makers failed and only one factory, H-D, could afford a team, which consisted of one man—Joe Petrali. That obviously wasn't fair.

So it came to happen that the AMA, which itself had been rescued from financial ruin by Harley and Indian when there weren't enough members to pay the office rent, drew up new rules. National championships would be decided on stock machines: *really* stock, no changes allowed, raced exactly as the bike came from the showroom, by the bike's owner. The only modifications permitted were removal of the lights, brakes, and license plate.

Tough but fair, as the umpire always says. The sporting machines in 1935 were the 45s, side-valve V-twins from Harley or Indian. There were a handful of imports, and one dealer was deeply involved in racing so the rules allowed 30ci overhead-valve engines to run against the larger, less efficient and heavier side-valvers.

The new class was called Class C, after A and B obviously, and a name yours truly has always lamented because it sounds like third class.

Which it wasn't. There were scores of racers who could buy a stock 45 and who wanted to race, so the fields came back and so did the crowds.

Compressing here, the Class C Harley began as the W series, introduced in 1937 with iron barrels and heads, three speeds forward via hand shift and foot clutch, rigid rear, and springer front, as described in chapter 11.

The WR simply did what the private buyer had had to do, that is, remove everything not needed for the actual race. Owner: Bob Shirey, Los Molinos, California.

Yes, shifting by hand was clumsy on the track, but the rules got around that, and protected the homeboys from foot-shifted imports . . . by having flat-track races run in top gear only.

By 1941, for the first time in motorcycle history, if you didn't win, it wasn't the fault of the factory or the rules. Fair racing is another component of good racing, and the WR made things fair.

As racing got closer and better and fiercer, the machines improved to the point of doing serious harm to the original idea. No villains or culprits named, but bikes were towed to the races and engine numbers were altered and the brakes and lights never came near the bike after the first meet.

So, in 1941, Harley-Davidson did the logical thing and introduced the WR, W for the 45 engine, R for racing. It was mostly the W model, in that it came with the separate engine, bore and stroke of 2.75x3.81in, side valves, and flat, alloy heads. The engine and gearbox were bolted to the frame, bridged by the primary drive and its housing. But the WR frame was of stronger and lighter steel, the valves and ports were larger, and the four one-lobe camshafts, set in an arc in the timing case, had extra lift and duration for optimum racing results.

Mostly, the WR was what the racer and dealer would have made for themselves out of the earlier WLDR, the full-road bike with racing

Front suspension is standard leading link. Front hub is spool, meaning no brake.

Side-valve 750cc WR engine used iron barrels and aluminum heads. Ignition is giant magneto, adapted from a tractor ignition, no kidding.

89

Rules required stock parts so tuners worked with variables. The front wheel here is 18in, with a wide tire for traction on a half-mile track. For the mile, where speed counts for more than traction, the rider would use a narrower 19in wheel.

parts. As an addition, the factory switched from a racing team to a racing department, with an engineer and helpers whose job it was to give aid and comfort to the Harley riders, to work with them instead of race against them. Some favored few got extra help, at the same time, so rivalries were fueled and the factory-versus-privateer struggle began and has continued ever since.

From a purely technical standpoint the WR didn't improve the breed. Instead, the WR's values began with the most basic. Anybody could buy one, from any Harley-Davidson dealership. And every part that could be used for racing was in the parts book, available over the counter on demand.

Next, the WR could be tailored. There were charts and boxes packed with engine, counter-shaft, and rear wheel sprockets and internal gearsets. There was a choice of 18 or 19in wheels.

There were spool hubs for the miles and half miles, where brakes were illegal, and drum brakes for the TTs (tourist trophy) and road races where brakes were needed. There were small gas and oil tanks for sprints, huge tanks for the longer events like Daytona Beach's 200 mile sand and asphalt race. American racing had evolved into a mix of racing forms unique to the world, and the WR could be adapted and equipped to compete in each of them. Think how that simplified the racer's life!

Best of all, each rider and tuner could work his magic without constraints. The rules said you had to begin with the stock heads and barrels and such. The owner or tuner was allowed to reshape said heads and barrels and revise the oiling systems and juggle the gears, all down the line. It made for what we'd now call a level playing field. That meant that the talent, which

isn't level as we all learn the hard way, could come out. Hard work and grit and creativity, as the first man who learned that bigger ports *aren't* always better discovered, could earn rewards. Which they did time and again.

It was a wonderful mix of freedom and equality. The example here, made in 1948 and owned since 1954 by retired expert Bill Shirey, is typical in that it's rigged for the half mile, with a 4.50x18in wheel and tire for traction: The mile needs less drag and traction and takes a 4.00x19in wheel and tire. The rear wheel has sprockets on both sides, so you can try one gearing and flop the wheel for a second choice. That's the normal flat-track tank and seat, with

the pad on the rear fender so the rider can slide back and tuck in. The paint is deep maroon simply because Shirey used to paint all his motorcycles, cars, and boat blue until his wife asked, why always blue? So the WR is maroon. He got the WR and kept it while racing professionally on KR Harleys and Nortons for no other reason than he always liked WRs.

Okay, by 1941 the WR wasn't advancing science, nor did it improve the motorcycle as transportation. And Harley-Davidson (along with Indian and the English brands) got some business for its efforts, so we aren't talking pure sport here.

Kickstart levers were carried, and folding footpegs, the better to not stab a fallen rider, were required.

Next page
Contrary to present practice, team race machines—which this one wasn't—were painted red rather than black and orange. High, wide handlebars are for leverage in the turns.

91

That doesn't matter. A good WR weighed 300lb and had 30-something horsepower and 110mph on tap. It was big and fast enough to challenge the best riders and win titles for the maker.

For the first time in motor racing history, if you didn't win, it wasn't the fault of the factory or the rules. Fair racing is another component of good racing, and the WR made things fair.

Generous fuel tanks were carried because in those days a national race on a mile track might go 100 miles.

93

Chapter 11

The W Series

'My Mom Wasn't Home That Day.'

Remember the Harley ad picturing the baby wrapped in the emblem and asking the question, "When did it start for you?"

For Grace McKean, it started when she was thirteen and her brother came home with an H-D 125, the tiddler introduced after World War II to bring new buyers into the postwar motorcycle market.

Grace was smitten. This was rural Illinois in the late 1940s and her mother was away for some reason, so she talked her brother into teaching her how to ride and she spent the next year or so putting around the tiny town and nearby roads, as free and independent as she'd always wanted to be.

So when Brother, who'd only used the bike for transportation, sold the little gem, Grace knew what her next move would be. She worked two jobs, took college courses to speed up her high school graduation, and on her seventeenth birthday she walked into the best Harley store in town and said she wanted the used bike in the back of the shop.

The dealer was a good man. No, he said, you don't want that old machine, that's for somebody who knows how to fix things. What you want is that shiny new blue job in the window.

Grace looked and sure enough, what she wanted more than anything in the whole world

was that bright blue 1951 WL. It was perfect on that day in 1951, and it's just as perfect forty years later. Yes, it's a one-owner bike.

Which brings us to the W series, the workhorses, pets, and perhaps even the seed corn of Harley's survival through the 1930s, across the war and into the present day.

The W series was nearly as basic as those first singles were. The first were produced in 1928, when the factory went practical, meaning they realized it was cheaper to provide power with a mid-size, 45ci side-valve engine than with less displacement but higher revs and complexity (read here overhead valves). And anyway, the side-valve Indians were at least equal to the ohv Harleys at the races. The first 45s were quite basic, with total loss oiling but with generators and wet batteries. In 1937, following the development of the ohv Model E, the 45 was named the W series and updated with dry sump, that is, recirculating oil delivery, while the smaller models got the modern styling and trim of the bigger twins.

In keeping with Harley practice, the W was the basic version, joined by the WL, with higher compression, and the WLD and WLDR, the more sporting bikes. Parallel to them came such diversities as the Servi-car, the three-wheeler used for courier service, for pickup and delivery

WL was the smaller Harley when the series began, but as the windshield and saddlebags illustrate, the enthusiastic owner could pile on the extras. Owner: Grace McKean, Chino, California.

Twin saddle tanks, hand shift, and a housing for the speedometer and ignition switch are between the tanks.

from service stations (when they used to give service), and by generations of cops handing out parking tickets.

Plus, the Army used fleets of adapted 45s, which were known as the WA, naturally. And late in the model run the factory admitted to what

had happened in racing and came out with the WR (see chapter 10), the stripped version of the WLDR that was full race with lights.

Okay. The first flathead 45 appeared in 1929 and the last Servi-car was made in 1974. True, there were major differences among the various

models, but the configuration was the same and a forty-five-year run proves its durability.

That and utility seem to have been the secret. To look at the WL is to believe that machines, too, have genes or at least some family traits. Just as those first production Harley-Davidsons were sturdier than their rivals in the teens, so were the W models built with extra strength. The Indian 45s were faster and lighter, but fragile to the point that many racing Indians were fitted with Harley lower ends, no kidding.

The W was basic: the standard H-D fork-and-blade connecting rods on assembled fly-wheels joined by a crankpin, 45deg included angle for the vee, and chain primary drive to a separate gearbox. Front suspension was springer forks, rear suspension was solid, and of course there was a hand shift and foot clutch on the left. The oil tank was one of the twin tanks on the frame backbone, which made it easy to fill while cutting down on gas capacity. And as perhaps the most basic of appeals, by this time you could get a Harley-Davidson that wasn't shiny olive drab (greenish brown). Even Ford caught on to bright colors before Harley-David-son did. Strange.

The W series had an underplayed appeal. All the recollections seem to begin with nega-

Headlights by this time were as good as those on cars.

Next page
Rails on the back of the buddy seat are so the shy passenger won't have to hug operator. Structure at rear is push-bar or bumper.

tives, as in the 45s weren't fast or light, and it took lots of stripping and modifying to keep up with the Indians. There were only three speeds and to keep the engine in the power band on top, you had to wind 'er out in second. Also, the steering wasn't as sharp as one might wish, and so on.

But all that didn't matter.

Using Grace McKean and her machine as evidence, the first appeal had to be that it looked just right. Beyond that, the W series models looked like their larger and faster siblings, the 61s and 74s.

Next, they were as reliable as anvils. Grace isn't very mechanical. In fact, she's actively un-mechanical. In the picture you can see a chromed toolbox aft of the gearbox on the right, right? Know what Grace keeps in there instead of tools? Her cosmetics, honest. Husband John twirls the wrenches, then? Nope. John rode a motorcycle once, in the Army. The sergeant said, Whatever you do, don't hit that post in the middle of the parade ground. So John promptly slammed into the post and hasn't ridden a motorcycle since. Grace puts in gas and oil and every few years asks Johnny Eagles to make sure the scoot's

WL engine shares all major parts with WR, except there's an ignition timer at the top of the timing case. The housing to the left of the rear cylinder head is the toolbox.

As exemplified here, the WL could go as far in one direction with the same design as the preceding WR went in the other.

working right. The odometer reads 71,000 miles. Ask about breakdowns, though, and Grace has to look up at the sky and think back.

Yes, she says, on one of the Death Valley runs back in the 1960s or so, the bike stopped. There was dirt in the fuel tank and it plugged the line. That's the only time her 45—Did you check the license plate, "My 45"?—has stopped running in forty years.

And we think reliability came to us from across the pond to our west.

In a recent issue of *American Heritage* magazine one of the editors deplored the notion that our times are always more complicated and difficult than earlier times.

An observer of history can only concur. Pictured here is one motorcycle, and its only owner.

The bike filled a need in her life, provided transportation, sport, friendship, and even a sense of belonging. You should hear what landladies thought of motorcycling women forty years ago!

The W series came out of a different time and place, no better or worse than now. Nostalgia is just as foolish as dismissal when it comes to history. Basic and strong, the 45 was perfectly designed to do the job, for the people who needed the job done.

Speaking of modern times, when the kids were grown, Grace got back into high annual mileage and John persuaded her to get a motorcycle with brakes, a Sportster in fact. She rides it and likes it.

But to see woman and machine in action, you'll have to look for Her 45.

As befits a machine that's been owned by the same person since new 40 years ago, a really personal plate.

Owner Grace McKean, on a day in the country.

Chapter 12

1952-1968 KR

The Side-valve Engine's Last Great Ride

Ready for flat track, the KR was Spartan, with rigid rear wheel and no brakes. Owner, Jeffrey S. Gilbert, Los Angeles, California.

As Winston Churchill would have said had he been lucky enough to report the races, the KR production racer ruled the tracks because so many worked so hard to get so much from such a feeble beginning.

Said feeble beginning was of course the Model K of 1952 (see chapter 13 for the details). For background here, suffice it to say that when the factory introduced a road bike displacing 750cc, it was inevitable that they'd also need a racing machine of the same displacement. That's probably in the reverse, however, in that 750 was the limit for national races and Harley-Davidson had been in the thick of the national championships for generations.

As we've also seen, H-D was perfectly capable of state-of-the-art racers as far back as 1916, and had been instrumental in shaping the production racer ideal, witness the WR series.

It all fell neatly into place. The K was a unit engine, valves in the barrels, a row of cams along the right side, four forward speeds. The K was a modern motorcycle with an engine slightly out of date and with a power output regretably modest for its size. Its good looks, hand clutch, foot shift, and full suspension put the K into contention with the imports and with the improvements detailed in the next chapter, made for a good sporting ride.

The racing KR was more (and less) of a problem.

The extra demand for it came because the other chaps were gaining. When Class C was invented back in the 1930s, there was only a handful of dealers handling imports and not many buyers for the trickle of bikes that came across the only pond then in use. Harley and Indian scrapped mostly with each other.

Indian was on the way out by 1952, but the war and prosperity had reinvented the sports bike and the imported option. Triumph and BSA and Norton and a few others were building dealer networks and selling lots of 500cc singles and twins. If they didn't invent the slogan "Win on Sunday, Sell on Monday," they surely knew what it meant.

So the KR was a useful blend of toolroom and production, old and new. The frame was a smaller version of the K, but made of better steel and less iron and with one major difference. Aft of the frame's rear corners, behind the seat and the rear engine mount, there were lugs. For the basic KR there was a subframe that bolted to the lugs and carried the rear wheel, rigidly mounted because dirt track in those days was still brakeless, on smooth cushion tracks, and the thinking was that compressing rear suspension used up power and subtracted from traction. (Historical

Tanks became smaller as races were shortened to 25 rather than 100 miles. Exhaust pipe length was a critical part of engine tuning. Tach drive is from the fitting on top of the timing case, where the ignition was on the WR and the road-going K models.

When the factory introduced a road bike displacing 750cc, it was inevitable that they'd also need a racing bike of the same displacement.

note here. Poor suspension design worldwide from the 1910s through the early 1950s made the idea of suspension seem worse than it was and delayed improvements for all those years.)

Like the eight-valve and WR racing engines, the KR powerplant used production parts and looked more production than it actually was. The AMA national rules then required that the machines be offered for sale to the public, in basic form and with options. It made sense in several ways for the KR to have the same basic engine cases, cylinders, gearbox, and so forth. In detail, the K/KR used a bore and stroke of 2.75x3.81in and displaced 45ci or 750cc, the limit, with some allowance for reboring. The engine was unit construction, primary drive on the rider's left, leading to a four-speed gearset housed behind the crankcase. It had a 45deg V-twin, built-up flywheels and crankpin, intake ports fed by a single carb inside the vee, and exhaust ports on the outside. And the valves were in the cylinders next to the bore and the piston, so the outgoing

A tachometer is the only instrument the rider has time to look at.

Rear axle mount adjusts for two reasons: First, to take up slack in the chain and second, because wheelbase is a way to tune the suspension. Riders moved the axle back and forth and added or subtracted chain to fit the new length.

Frame has double front downtube, single tube backbone, and ends at the rear engine mount and seat mount. There's a subframe for the rear wheel.

and incoming charges followed a tricky and restricted path, in and out, up and over.

The basic design was pure logic. Did the job, as the saying goes. Just as good was the list of options. Because there were road races and TTs, dirt track with jumps and turns in both directions, brakes and suspension were good to have

sometimes. The KR frame came with the lugs and subframe for dirt because there was a second system, shock absorbers and a swing arm, that attached to the same lugs and voila! rear suspension. Drum brakes could be fitted to the hubs front and rear, you could have 18 or 19in wheels, and there were literally pages of gearsets and

sprockets listed in the catalog, which not incidentally also had the dimensions for the various bolts needed to fasten the parts together. A normal fuel tank came with the early KRs, then the peanut tank from the Hummer was used for short races, and there were five- and six-gallon tanks, along with different seats and bars, for the road races.

Might also mention here that the ideal, unique to American motorcycle racing as far as research shows, was that anybody with a competition license—earned by doing well in the lesser classes which also is an ideal—could buy a racing machine and all the parts and by juggling said parts could ride that one bike in short track, miles, and half miles, TT and road events, and become national champion. No factory contract, no secret source of parts had to be gained or overcome.

We are approaching the important part. When the AMA—more accurately the guys from Harley and Indian who stepped in to save the AMA and professional racing during the Depression—drew up the production class rules, they sincerely meant to be fair. They called for production parts because the handful of factory guys with racing parts had made pro racing a joke, a monopoly. They set the limits as 750cc side-valve, 500cc overhead-valve because that's what the sporting semi-pro, domestic, or import-mounted, rode.

I mention this because the motorcycle press later created the legend that the mean old Ammurican factories rigged the rules so the furriners didn't have a chance. It wasn't so. There were isolated incidents of chicanery and some truly dumb officiating now and again but the fact is, the equivalency rules worked and made for

Magneto is at lower left, where the generator was on the road machines, with drive from the cam gears. Carburetor is behind the big air cleaner, used on the dusty tracks of the time. The oil tank is behind the rear cylinder.

107

good racing, and the open-parts-counter policy did enable the outsiders to meet and beat the official teams, Yank or Brit.

Best of all, the rules inspired wizardry.

Sit back and imagine the workings of the side-valve engine. Most obvious, the intake and exhaust tracts are tortuous. The KR used a special valvetrain with the valves inclined toward the bore instead of parallel, a better angle of attack. But even so, getting air and fuel in and out of a flathead is never easy.

Next, compression ratio. Increasing the squeeze has always been the best and easiest way to improve power and efficiency.

But you can't do much squeezing to a flat-head. Make the combustion chamber smaller atop the piston and you ruin the path for the heated charge to expand, that is, push down. Make the space smaller above the valves and there's no room for the valves to open, or for the charge to flow.

Higher isn't better. In contrast, what the side-valve tuner has to go after is the optimum compression ratio, the ratio of total displacement to combustion chamber size that's the perfect mean between squeeze and ease of flow.

I don't have to tell you that this perfection is elusive. All I have to say is that for seventeen years, the best minds in motorcycle racing worked on the problem and they picked a horse-power or two every year, 38bhp for the factory bikes in the early 1950s, 62 to 64 by 1968 or 1969.

They did it by degrees making nearly imperceptible changes here and there. The steps came in stages. First, there was the stock engine, as sold to the qualified public. Then came the official modifications, in a book prepared by the racing department. It listed all the parts and changes to be made, how to work out the best gearing and so forth, and it came with detailed machining and assembly instructions for putting this wisdom into metal.

The secret here was, it was almost all self-discovered secrets. The factory's advice would put you into the ballpark, assuming you understood the instructions and followed them perfectly. Beyond that, the winner's circle was a matter of how much more you could learn beyond the factory level. Remember, all the parts from which the winners were made were for sale. This probably stifled major innovation, but it also created a group of private tuners who were at least the factory team's equals.

And they gloried in it. Tom Sifton, Len Andres, and Ralph Berndt, among others, had the most fun doing things their own way.

During the eighteen years the KR reigned as the official machine, the national championship was won five times by imports, five times by factory-backed Harley riders . . . and eight times by riders—namely Joe Leonard, Brad Andres, and Carroll Resweber—who rode for private tuners Sifton, Berndt, and Len Andres.

Having one make and model didn't interfere. There were the factory bikes, painted pepper red. There were the guys from Ohio, who painted their machines yellow and had such prestige that riders from other states copied the color in hopes of bluffing their rivals. Berndt meanwhile painted his bikes blue and left out the brand name to the extent that Walter Davidson, who came through with backing now and then, used to pointedly ask what make Berndt's KR was.

There's a chance that some of the excitement and rivalry conveyed in accounts of those days came in part because the reporters were fans and were creating heroes. It's possible. But I—and I inject here that your aged scribe was too young to have seen the KRs in action—doubt it. My bet is, the close and fair racing took place because there were clear and basic rules, used in a context with which all parties agreed.

Further, they worked because the motorcycle itself worked. The KR was a synergistic miracle. When overhead-valve engines appeared in other circles, car racing for instance, the rules had to be changed so the old crocks could stay in the running.

In 1969 the AMA rules were changed: still production based, still 750cc limit, but with no restriction on valve systems or even on the number of cylinders.

The Brits were primed. They had Gary Nixon, a scrapper from the git-go, and they gave him a choice of twin or triple ohv Triumph. They rented the long (1¹/₈mi) track at Nazareth, Pennsylvania, prior to the national, so they could get the gearing and suspension right. Nixon had won the national title for Triumph in 1967 and 1968, so he was the defending champion. He picked the triple and ran on the record with it.

But in the race, H-D teamster Fred Nix, on an outmoded, rigid-rear frame KR powered by an engine two generations out of date, won by nearly half a mile.

Now *that* is a finest hour.

The basic design was pure logic. Did the job, as the saying goes. Just as good was the list of options.

Chapter 13

KHK

Innocence Vanquished, Faith Defended

Nothing lends itself to arrogance quite as well as hindsight.

Even drop-outs from Parking Attendant College could have figured that when World War II ended, there would be an explosion of social, economic, and political forces, a whole new world you could say. Every executive and engineer with enough sense to pour rainwater into a flowerpot began planning for the end of the war, before it happened.

Even so, implementing the best-laid plans takes time. Peace arrived in 1945, but it wasn't until 1949 that the truly new cars came out of Detroit, or Coventry. (The Germans needed a bit more time, for reasons we needn't bother with here, while the Japanese were still copying Harley and BMW except for a racer who was fiddling with bicycles and surplus engines. A guy named Honda. Watch this space.)

The hindsight arrives for us with motorcycles. Indian had survived the war, had some capital to invest, and decided to keep on with the big twins and expand by making what amounted to copies of the English bikes, ohv vertical twins and singles with all the improvements, as in full suspension. (The program wasn't a success, indeed contributed to the demise of Indian several years later, but that's another tragedy.)

As is traditional, Harley's bold postwar venture was launched with one foot firmly planted in survival. At the top of the line there was the Knucklehead in 61 and 74ci form, springer front and rigid rear, hand shift and foot clutch, and starting by kick and grunt. For the kids, as noted earlier, there was the Model S two-stroke, a radical departure from previous Harleys but mostly a borrowed design.

The major change came to the middle-weight-class bike in the form of the Model K.

A first glance showed lots of homework had been done, and done right. In overall concept the K was thoroughly modern, with telescopic forks suspending the front and a swing arm with shocks handling the rear wheel, this when the rival English makes and Indian were still struggling with sprung hubs and other horrors.

The clutch operated by the left hand, and shifting was done with the right foot. Repeat, the right foot, just like the limey bikes and on the Indian side, despite Harleys having shifted on the left since they first began shifting at all. Sales and marketing had shown what the buyers bought: 40 percent of the market was imports early in the 1950s. The controls were clearly modified to meet and beat the competition.

Styling was a clean mix, slick and trim most places but with a large (4.5gal) fuel tank and

KHK was the best of the K series, with a modern chassis, telescopic forks, swing arm rear suspension and unit engine, but with side valves against the ohv rivals. Owner: Brad Andres, San Diego, California.

buckhorn bars, echoing the FL big twin the K buyer was presumed to admire. The two looks blended nicely, though, and the K was obviously as modern as it looked.

Except that the powerplant was a new and improved version of the W series. Same bore and stroke, same row of four one-lobe cams on the right side, same system—there were few if any actually shared parts—of valves in the barrels, that is, side valves. The barrels were iron and the heads aluminum, the single carb sat to the left of the 45deg vee and the exhausts were on the outside of the vee, on the right and merged aft of the seat.

The difference, and the most modern touch of all, was unit construction. The flywheels and crankpin were in a front cavity, the primary drive was in a compartment on the left, and the gears and cams were housed on the right, with the four-speed gearbox in its own cavity behind the flywheels, and all the parts and components in or on two halves of a common case. No more engine and gearbox mounted separately in the frame, no more misaligned primary drives. Neat, and once

Rear hub carried the drum brake inboard of the sprocket. Lower shock mount was mid-swing arm, which gave too much leverage from the wheel against the arm, which flexed.

Voltage regulator is black box at lower left, air cleaner is at right, and accessory horn is between them.

112

All the KHK's improvements—the increased compression ratio, polished ports, and hot cams—were internal, but they made the model a match for the imported competition.

Ignition timer mounts atop timing case. The arm and wire on the timer rotate it and advance and retard spark timing, from the left grip. Kick the engine over with spark advanced, and it kicks back. Few owners needed more than one kick to learn the lesson.

again in advance of the rivals from here and there.

In management's defense, there's nothing actually wrong with side valves and flat heads. Harley-Davidson had years of experience with the design and the practice. The engineers knew the system and while there were teething troubles with the first Ks, they weren't in the engine.

Thing was, the K wasn't very fast. It wasn't as fast as it looked. And it wasn't as fast as the sporting English 500s. And even though Ford and Plymouth were still using side-valve engines, they were prewar designs, soon to be replaced with ohv. The newest Harley was out of date the day it appeared.

This is side hindsight, as it were, but years later it turned out there had been an ohv project on the drawing boards at the time. However, the wider vee and new heads and cam system took too long to produce and cost too much, so the company opted to go with the K. It wasn't that they didn't know the flathead was obsolete.

Not that anybody took comfort from this at the time. The K looked fine, handled acceptably at least, . . . and was slow. The first cure was a

Unit engine displaced 54ci in the KH and KHK versions, and was obviously based on the preceding W series. Big fuel tank and nacelle for the headlight show influence of the larger F models.

Cooling fins for the cylinder heads were elaborate and gave extra fin area to handle the extra power and heat.

factory-installed hop-up kit, the cams and valves from the racing-only KR, with lower and more sporting handlebars. The KK, as the model was known, was closer to the competition, but not enough.

The more sensible approach to the lack of punch came for model year 1954, when the stroke was increased, from 3.8125 to 4.56in. That's a lot, and it took displacement from 45 to 54ci. Claimed power went from 30 to 38bhp. The larger engine justified larger valves, which is one reason power went up a shade more than the displacement did. Nor did the larger engine require more weight, so the KH was faster than the K and could come closer to the lighter (and smaller, be fair) imports.

But it still wasn't a machine to quicken the sporting blood. In 1955 and 1956, Harley-Davidson laid the groundwork for the Superbike, which is why the model is included here.

The name was KHK. By now the discerning reader will know that this means the K engine, with some extra power as in H, dating back to the VLH, and with the second K indicating a higher state of tune.

The KHK was a sports kit. We have to step carefully here because Harleys have always been offered with extras, such as windshields, saddlebags, chrome covers for the kick-lever spring, and so forth. Harley buyers have also had the option to substitute certain items, such as larger or smaller fuel tanks, or reverse gear and lower gearing to work with a sidecar.

But the KHK came as, or was billed in the catalog as, a kit. This meant you could get your KHK with all the other extras and/or accessories, bags, case guards, and the like, and with the high bars and big tank. This probably helped the buyer since there are guys who want extra power and a windshield for the power to push. But it also made things less impressive because you had to *show* the other chaps that you had the hot number, meaning impressive and illegal displays of speed, as they say when they write you up a ticket.

But that's minor. What mattered first was that the KHK came from the factory with the hot cams and valves developed for the KR, and with some handwork improving the parts and valve seats. In 1955 and 1956, this was enough to give Harley-Davidson something that could run with the other big dogs (as the saying goes, sit on the porch if you can't run with the big dogs).

Second, and much more subtle, *there weren't many KHKs around.*

Legend, remember? Would the Ferrari GTO be priced at millions of bucks now if Fiat had produced, say, 100,000 examples? Surely not. Becoming a legend requires that not everybody have access to the treasure or the facts.

With the KHK, Harley-Davidson explored the sports market. The public wasn't ready. The imports, most of which were sporting, did very well in the middleweight class, while in 1956 Harley-Davidson sold 714 KHKs, according to the factory's skimpy records, versus 2,219 two-stroke singles and 5,786 big twins.

What the KHK did outsell was the plain KH, of which 539 were produced that model year.

What this meant in the long run was that the salespeople who took notes would notice, and would—as we'll see shortly—listen to the savvy dealers who took notes. The motorcycle was being reinvented, and it would be reborn as a sport vehicle.

In the short run, for those with tiddler two-strokes and Cushman Eagles, or with tired old big twins, or even with a slightly secondhand K model which the riders of Triumph Tigers loved to see at stop lights, somewhere out there was the

fabled KHK, and when they'd saved their money or lucked out, why, they'd put those upstarts in their places.

The KHK didn't win races, nor did it return H-D to health and profit.

What it did was keep the dream alive.

Switches, speedometer, and steering damper are mounted to the top clamps of the fork tubes.

Chapter 14

XLCH

Harley Invents the Superbike

The ohv XL engine wasn't nearly as much like the side-valve K and W powerplants as it looked. Magneto ignition mounts where the plain XLH and the older Ks had their timers.
Owner: Randy Janson, El Cajon, California.

Overleaf
Harley-Davidson has always excelled at mix and match: If you took the KR and the KHK and blended their looks, you'd have a race bike in the legal minimum of street clothing . . . and you'd have the XLCH.

The secret password for the success story of the XLCH is either savvy or serendipity, depending on the side from which you're looking.

The story begins in 1957, when H-D introduced the Sportster. The new model's ancestry was clearly the K and KH, with the same basic frame and suspension and brakes and drivetrain configuration, to the point that several parts in the clutch, primary, and gearbox interchanged.

But the engine was much newer than it looked. Mostly, it had overhead valves! At last, a design that could match the English twins, rocker for rocker. And the Harley design was a classic, two big valves inclined at nearly a right angle, housed in a domed combustion chamber above a slightly domed piston. A hemispherical chamber, as they called it then, just like Chrysler and Offenhauser and all the other racers used.

Equally modern was the reduced stroke and bigger bore. The new engine, lettered XL, was nominally the same displacement as the replaced KH, at 54ci. But the XL had a shorter stroke, 3.8125in (right, same as the old K) and a bore of 3in, so the ohv engine could rev higher, safer, and take advantage of better breathing while the larger bore meant larger valves, for the same reason.

Oddly, there never was a plain X model as there was a J, W, K, and F. Standard practice for

The Motor Company had been to use one letter, followed by the engine letter and the tuning letter, WL, FL, and such. But the first year of the Sportster, a great name by the way and cast into the primary cover in 1957, had rather a low compression ratio of 7.5:1, and the letters XL.

Now we come to the two opposing views of the story. We've seen from the KHK that management, sales, and engineering had no problem with hotter versions of the basic package. We know from history that motorcycles were sport machines and there was lots of racing, sanctioned and otherwise.

It makes sense, then, to follow the official factory history and accept the tuned version from marketing surveys or similar sources, all well reasoned and planned.

Well, folklore—and we're speaking now of people who were there—tells it differently.

Cycle magazine tested the XL in March 1957 and noted that the new model was "designed primarily with an eye for the touring motorcyclist." So it appears, with the four-gallon tank and big headlight nacelle like that on the FL. And an ad in the same issue lists forty features, including a loud horn, big tank, sturdy brake rod, and, no kidding, a mellow muffler.

In February 1958, the company advertised the Sportster H, as in XLH, with larger ports and

intake valves and a compression ratio of 9:1, but the model shown has lights and even case guards.

What the ads *didn't* tell us was that when the XL was introduced to the dealers, several of the sharper guys, former racer turned dealer Sam Arena for one, said that the bike was nice, but what about sport? What about something the dealer could sell to the amateur racer, for the woods and deserts?

The executives didn't think much of the idea. But they were fair men and offered to build such a version if the California crowd would promise to order at least 100 examples.

They did. And the factory came through with a stripper, the same XL frame and engine but without lights or horn or even a battery. There was a solo seat, a tiny fuel tank borrowed from the two-stroke single, and instead of the ignition timer there was a real magneto, perched atop the timing case and ready to deliver the same sparks and grief as the KR racers got.

The record gets confused here, but from the scant evidence collected, we know there were

The red caps cover the ends of the shafts on which the rocker arms ride. They are for style only and don't, alas, have lights inside. Chromed cover for stock horn fills the vee on the left as the carb and air cleaner do on the right.

119

several hundred stripped XLs built and sold, mostly in 1958. The ads of the day show the model and call it the XLC.

Okay. The idea came from the California dealers, and that's where the bikes went at first and it's my bet, backed up by the old-timers, that C stood for California.

The XLC got the attention it deserved and this time the factory reckoned they could do even better if the thing had some claim to road use.

Thus, early in 1958, Harley-Davidson combined the stripped XLC, inspired by the dealers, and the beefed engine from the XLH . . . and called it the XLCH.

We're going into all this because when the XLH was introduced, some clever ad writer decided to say H stood for Hot. And a few years after that the same wiseacre said CH meant Competition Hot, and lazy reporters ever since have picked that up as gospel and it ain't. Competition Harleys have R in their designations and C has stood for Classic or even Custom I believe, while H designates Heavy Duty, if anything; refer back to the chapter on the VLH for further querulous details.

Back to the XLCH.

Harley-Davidson had invented the Superbike.

Not the sports bike, nor the fast bike, nor even the high-performance bike. The XLCH was like a P-47 or a prewar Ford with a bored-out Mercury V-8, never mind that a 707 cruised faster or a Duesenberg had more rated power.

The XLCH looked the part. The stock tank was tiny, the fenders were smaller, and the bars lower, and in some years the pipes were high down the sides. The bulging housing for the headlight used to make the XLH look like a junior FLH, but was replaced with a miniature light, the legal minimum, clamped to an odd sort of bracket barely held by the upper clamps. And the pipes were as close to open as the law allowed . . . this was before the federal government took over vehicle design, by the way.

What the XLCH looked and sounded like was the proverbial .38 Special in a .22 frame.

Better still, that's how it acted.

The CH was fast, faster than the H, and the FLH, and all the stock imported twins. The details varied from year to year and from magazine to magazine, but in general, during the CH's peak, the early and mid-1960s, you could count on easily topping 100mph off the showroom floor,

120

Previous page
Given some work and a good day, a brave rider could make the speedometer honest.

Narrow profile and miniature headlight suit the style of the machine.

or turning the standing quarter mile in the low fourteens. Strip off the road stuff and you pared off 20 or 30lb. Might also mention that in full road trim a CH weighed 475 to 495lb, only 20 to 40lb more than the 650s from England.

Funny thing about reading old magazines. The figures change, but the superlatives remain the same. It's true that in 1992 the performance motorcycles from the 1960s don't seem to handle all that well, and in fact they probably didn't.

But the riders of the day didn't have the future to compare it against and in context, the XLCH was pretty good, good enough to give good performance on the open road, in the mountains, and even in desert races, speaking of things past we can't imagine doing now.

The XLCH was strong. The KH had a longer stroke in the same case dimensions, so stroked flywheels were a simple machine shop project. There was also a competition Spor tster, the XLR. That model provided useful research into valves and cams and porting and getting the beast to hold together. The XLCH became something of a cult motorcycle at the drags and the flats and even in road races, when the rules didn't exclude the monster. There are more Sportsters in the record books than big twins, and you can mention that the next time you hear Arlen Ness refer to the Sportster as the Paperboy Bike, which he

does just because Big Twin guys like to needle the babybike crowd.

Probably the most subtle virtue the CH had was that it really was a beast. Didn't take to neglect and when it blew, the pieces were still falling the next week. Even in good health it could be a bitch to start, something usually blamed on the magneto, with good reason.

(*Hot Rod* magazine's test said the engine was difficult to start, but they could do it once they'd been taught how. *Motor Cycling* magazine in England noted that "starting from cold was difficult and demanded observance of a critical drill . . . the knack was not completely acquired during the test period." Having been there, I vote with *Motor Cycling*.)

Sorry to say, the legend of the XLCH sort of fades away. The XL series got electric start, the feds and states imposed rules on controls and noise, and surely the killer was the arrival of threes and fours from across the pond.

But that needn't detract from the CH's accomplishments. Would the others have gone the power route if they hadn't been shown that it was worth the effort?

And anyway, we can give the last word to those most difficult to impress, the hard-kicking writers from *Motor Cycling*: The XLCH "produced in several hardened critics enthusiasm which was only just this side of idolatry."

The CH was fast, faster than the H and the FLH, and all the stock imported twins. In general, you could count on easily topping 100mph off the showroom floor.

Chapter 15

The Panhead

Great Leaps and No Kicks

Massive fork legs taper toward the axle, a polished cover fills the side of the hub that doesn't have a brake, and the front fender seems almost overprotective of the tire. Owner: Museum of Flying Auction, Santa Monica Airport, California.

Overleaf
Last of the Panheads came in 1965, by which time the big twins had telescopic forks, swing arm rear suspension, foot shift, and hand clutch, all done in careful, gradual steps.

When the staff of *Road & Track* magazine, pontificators to a man and woman, debated the question of what was the most important technical development in the history of the automobile, they went through all the fancy stuff that comes first to mind, as in turbocharging and electronic ride control and air bags and such, and when the votes were in the winner was . . . electric starting.

With what now seems so basic, the car became more accessible to twice as many people, with a touch of the button.

It was a similar story for the 1965 FLHE. As you could infer, the FLH means heavy-duty big twin and the E stands for electric leg; yes, there is still a kick lever in the usual place. Motorcyclists are leery of change and often rightly so.

But today, the 1965 big twin is celebrating what has to be a record for time in service. In its eighteen years on the job, the version of Harley's big twin known as the Panhead saw more major change than the company or the sport, never mind the model, had seen in motorcycling's history. It perfectly illustrates how Harley-Davidson does things.

Starting point once again was the end of World War II. The original overhead-valve design for the 61 and later 74 worked well enough, but it was prone to oil leaks and sometimes overheated.

The engineers took a bold step, perhaps because much had been learned about metal and casting during the war, and redid the twin's cylinder heads. They were cast in aluminum alloy rather than iron and there was a new valvetrain, with enclosed oil lines and completely covered rockers and springs. The other bold move was to equip the valvetrain with hydraulic dampers, using oil pressure to make the push between cam lobe and rocker arm, with no need for working clearance and thus with no clatter.

As any Harley historian would predict, there was trouble at first. The changes were clearly improvements and once management had decided to call the engine the Panhead, named after the cake-pan-looking rocker covers, not many people objected to the new top end. The hydraulic lifters failed at a high rate, though, and it required moving the actual hydraulic portions from the head to the case, just above the camshaft instead of a long way above, to make them work right.

What they had mostly was a top-end swap, with the same engine cases and gearbox and with 61 and 74ci versions, still labeled E and F, respectively. The Panhead engine(s) went into a frame with rigid rear wheel and springer front end, foot clutch, and hand shift. The new top end was enough for one year, in other words.

126

In model year 1949, the big twins got a new front end, with hydraulic, telescopic forks. This wasn't radical; most of the motorcycle companies worldwide were doing the same thing at about the same time, but it did keep H-D current. (It also makes one wonder, seeing that the telescopic forks have done so well for so many for so long, why some people were willing to retrofit with the springer front suspension now in vogue.)

Speaking of being in step, in 1952 the Panheads got foot shift and hand clutch, again like the other makes. This was in tune with the new Model K, the middleweight, and with the imports except that first, the F and E models had the levers on the left, and the K and imports had levers on the right. Second, because bikers don't like to have change forced on them, you could still get hand shift and foot clutch for the big bikes if you wanted it that way. And 1952 was the last year for the 61, as the 74 and the K had the small big twin, so to speak, bracketed.

Restorers need reminding that in 1955 the factory jacked up the new heads, you could say, and slid a new lower end beneath them. The Panhead top did run cleaner and cooler and used less oil and because of that, the engine could be tuned to give more power. To take advantage of that, the lower end got better bearings and cases. In keeping with other remarks on the designa-

Towering windshield was a special favorite of the touring crowd. Twin fishtail mufflers and tailpipes are mostly for symmetry, as the rear cylinder feeds the muffler on the left *and* the right.

Cakepan aspect of the valve covers gave rise to the engine's nickname. Timer is the angled object parallel to the front pushrod covers. Monster battery, hidden here by the huge chrome panel, didn't preclude the fitting of the good old step-starter.

tions, the top-line engine, the one with the most power, was called the FLH. There was no more F, by the way, as even the basic package came with a medium high-compression ratio.

Darn, almost forgot. When the new front suspension was fitted, the model got a new name, actually one of the first times a Harley model ever had a formal name: Hydra-Glide, with a hyphen, just like Harley-Davidson.

This trivia is included because in 1958 the rigid rear wheel was replaced with a swing arm and springs and shocks. There were—and probably still are—those who said that with the big

tires and sprung seat, you didn't need rear suspension. Don't believe it.

The second suspension brought with it a new name, Duo-Glide, which surely needs no more explanation.

The last big leap was in 1965 and was, as anybody could predict, electric starting. This required a conversion to 12 volts and a larger battery and that brought with it some relocation of other parts and, of course, the starter itself weighed a good amount. There was also some work that needed to be done after the first examples were sold to the public.

Big was both better and beautiful in 1965, so extras like caseguards and luggage racks, atop the rear fender, were provided as a matter of course.

Police style seat was shaped for the human seat, and is one of the best ever put on a motorcycle.

None of which mattered worth a hoot. Probably because the Japanese had always considered the motorcycle a utility vehicle, as opposed to the western notion of sport being the primary concern, the Oriental products had come with electric legs from nearly the beginning. By 1965 there were hundreds of thousands of people who knew that you could own a motorcycle that started on command, hot or cold, and no intricate drill required. The Americans and the Europeans had to follow that lead, even if—as happened—they didn't get the hang of the operation for a generation or two.

Fair play, here. Nothing you can do with boots on is as satisfying as kick-starting a big bike—when it works. The rest of the crowd, wimps one and all, push a button and look sheepish while you, the pro, retard the spark or give two priming kicks with the switch off, or whatever the ritual is. You leap into the air, straighten your leg, and "BAROOM!" the mighty powerplant roars to life and you pretend not to

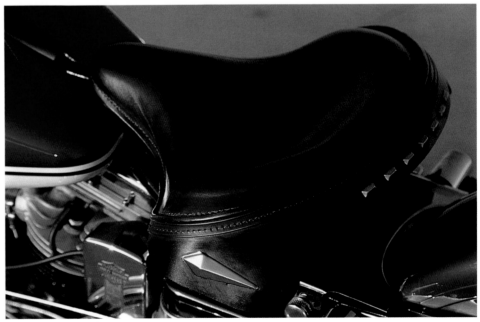

The twin tanks are separate metal structures, but they're joined by hidden tubing beneath the frame and tank bodies.

Next page
Primary case and cover, between the engine and gearbox on the bike's lower left, has grown a bulge to accommodate the electric starter and its gears.

know the others wish they had your skill and expertise.

That's when it works.

When it doesn't, you kick until you sweat through your jacket. Then your wife kicks till her legs quiver, and then you enlist the help of a couple of guys who can't hide their snickers, and they push you across the parking lot and if you're lucky, it goes gag-wheeze-pop-baroom. You mumble something about hot cams or too much compression. You fool nobody.

Kick starting means you know what you're doing.

Electric starting means you know the engine will start.

And that's why the FLHE, the 1965 Panhead, was a peak of achievement for H-D.

The solid base for this peak was a foundation of steady improvement. From first to last, the Panhead illustrates how Harley-Davidsons not only progressed, but kept from getting too far ahead of itself, or the buyers.

John R. Bond, spiritual founder of *Road & Track* magazine, worked as an engineer at Har-

ley right after the war. He remained a fan all his life. He used to reflect on his time at H-D and recalled his fascination with the large number of innovative and creative ideas tested within the factory walls, and the small number of same that emerged.

With good reason. We've mentioned Indian's disastrous venture into middleweights. Later we'll see the English collapse as they imitate the Japanese, and even the Japanese will take a beating overextending themselves. In the middle, Harley-Davidson took careful steps. There were some difficulties with the first Pans, but the lower end and chassis were tested and determined solid. The first telescopic forks weren't right, but chassis and engine were; the rear suspension needed work but the front didn't. And so it went, something old, something new, and yeah, a couple of things borrowed.

By 1965, with electrics up to state of the art, the Harley big twin was grown up, solid, and dependable, and ready for the people who simply wanted to go for a long ride.

Chapter 16

FLH

Long Lives the King of the Road

Don't read this chapter yet. First, look at the 1969 FLH pictured in profile. If you're old enough to vote and young enough to still care about voting, odds are this profile has spelled motorcycle for you since you were too young to spell m-o-t-o-r-c-y-c-l-e.

There are several reasons for this.

During the 1960s, motorcycles weren't popular with the general public. They were used mostly by motor officers, that is, cops. Indian had departed and the patrol options for Moto Guzzi and Kawasaki et al. weren't on the market yet. Thus, when you saw a motorcycle, it was in your mirror or next to you and the red light was on; people remember sights like that.

Next and probably not entirely least, Harley-Davidson and the company's customers used this popularity to evolve the big twin into the touring bike.

The first of these steps came in 1966, with the arrival of still another new top end for the venerable big V-twin. The name game had been established by then. Look at the right side of the FLH's engine shown here and you can see that the cake-pan-shaped rocker covers have been replaced by rocker boxes that look like the back of a coal or snow shovel, hence the nickname Shovelhead.

The heads were done in the same general design as those for the XL (Sportster) engine, except that the 74 heads were done in alloy and the 883's were in iron. (Nobody knows why, any more than they know why one engine was named in cubic inches and the other in cubic centimeters. And while we're on that subject, the official name had become Electra Glide, without a hyphen, never mind that it's always Harley-Davidson.)

The new heads were cleaner and stronger and flowed more air and produced more power, which was safe because of the stronger lower end that ushered in the FLH option. The rating was 60bhp, five up on the last Panhead, although the larger battery and starter added weight and the weight meant other parts were beefed up which added more weight, and the new machine wasn't any quicker than the older ones. It would haul all the gear, which is what counted.

About that gear: Ever since the first brave souls rode out of town with clouds in the sky, Harley and rivals have offered options. Way back then, there were cloaks and leggings and cloth and isinglass windshields and leather saddlebags and so forth, along with extra lights and toolboxes and more chrome than you can look at with both eyes open.

Sidecars haven't been a major part of motorcycling since the arrival of cheap four-wheelers, but they still have a charm all their own. Harley-Davidson has never forgotten that. Owner: Gwen Hansen, Ventura, California.

Saddlebags, sidecar body, and two rear fenders fill the spaces and give lots of places to put lights.

Harley-Davidson's fiberglass company—and the resulting in-house expertise—let the company be one of the few motorcycle makers to supply its own sidecars.

Fiberglass was the material of the future in the late 1960s and one of H-D's subsidiaries used the stuff to make golf carts. This led to expertise and expansion . . . you noticed the sidecar, eh?

Hard to imagine not noticing a sidecar. Since back when automobiles came without tops, a few hardy souls have preferred adding a third wheel to one side of a two-wheeler. Sidecars, or more properly termed combinations, are machines apart from the rest. They don't act like four-wheelers, and they surely don't act like bikes.

But there are those who like them. The combination shown here is the property of Gwen Hansen, and in case anybody wants to say they didn't offer Harleys in candy red and white in 1969, know that the colors are there because the rig was a Christmas present from husband Dave. Gwen isn't a big woman. She likes the FLH better than any other make or model, but it's difficult for her to heave the big bike off the stand or hold it up, hence the chair. It's used every day, incidentally.

Sidecars have been an option since the oldest employees can't remember. They were so much a part of the catalog that you could get four speeds forward or three forward and one reverse as a normal option until 1977.

But that wasn't the only place fiberglass was used. H-D (among others) realized that the material was a fine replacement for cloth and

Ignition and light switch made use of the convenient space atop the twin tanks.

135

Rocking lever for gearshift lets you step down with your toe for downshifts, step down with your heel for upshifts, and keeps your boots unscuffed. Black box above primary cover is the oil tank.

One of the FLH's options, along with the sidecar of course, was reverse gear, three forward and one back where the single-track bikes had four forward.

leather, which led to the creation of stowage boxes—we'll call them saddlebags, although they really aren't—attached to the rear fender, and larger boxes above the fender. (Fiberglass was used for other body parts as well; see chapter 17 for details on the boatback Super Glide.)

In 1966, first year of the Shovelhead, Harley-Davidson invented the touring package, in the guise of bags and fairing offered together. In 1969 the theme was taken to its logical conclusion, with the side boxes, a top box, and a fairing. Fiberglass, naturally.

The fairing went beyond classic. It was made by an outside team, and bolted to the bars and fork tubes. Science says fairings should be on the frame rather than the parts that steer, but the King of the Road fairing, as they called it then, never noticed. It was big and wide and fended off wind and rain and provided such a pocket of still air that there were riders who cruised across country smoking cigarettes: try that on a bare bike.

Parallel to this, Harley's big twin had floorboards while most everybody else had footpegs.

Brilliant paint didn't come from the factory. Instead, the combination was a Christmas present from the owner's husband, so the rig was painted in Christmas colors.

Proper size headlight was supplemented by two smaller versions, known in the catalog as passing lights. Fat, low pressure tire makes wide bars welcome.

The FLH inherited big, wide, low-pressure tires from the time of no suspension. For the same reason the seat, styled like the one on Grandpa's tractor, was suspended via spring and damping, on a vertical post housed in the frame.

Distinct, is what the FLH was. It didn't work or ride like anything else, nor did it work like anything else. When you were on the highway, driving in the role of Mom or Dad or standing on the rear seat looking out the back and making faces like Junior or Sis, when you saw or heard a motorcycle, what you saw or heard was an FLH.

Mostly because it was *the* big motorcycle and well known to the general public, chaps in the know tended to make jokes or assume the FLH had nothing to offer them. When I edited a motomag (*Cycle World*, to be exact), on two occasions I conned non-Harley types into riding an FLH. One was a desert racer and English fan, the other a road racer with Italian involvement. Both took a short hop and laughed; then after a week on the road they came back converts, to the extent that they wondered why they'd been so slow to appreciate the Big Twin.

What made it special?

My favorite was the saddle. It was shaped just right, with the rider sitting up and nicely balanced in the middle of the seat, and the bike.

With that came posture. The motor officers knew their ergonomics when they specified Bolt Upright. The FLH's controls had your hands, feet, back, and neck where they'd be comfortable all day. With the fairing or windshield you had no wind to fight, so you sat there and admired the passing scenery. With bare bars you adopted the Million Mile Slouch, a relaxed slump into the wind, so you were balanced and relaxed . . . and looked the part. Some of us, okay me, used to practice looking as if we'd been riding much longer than a seventeen-year-old could have ridden.

Until the feds interfered, the FLH had no throttle spring. Set it and forget it. Yes, like brakeless racing it sounds much scarier and trickier than it actually was.

Then there's ride and handling. This is deduction, but the suspended seat presumably made up for the lack of wheel travel in the actual suspension, and the lack of wheel travel made handling predictable. FLH steering was slow and sure, undisturbed by ruts or bumps. The big tires helped here, too. One of my brightest FLH memories was riding gravel roads in Norway, dragging the floorboards and sliding the rear wheel while a hotshot pal on a dropped-bars Yamaha triple got smaller in the mirrors. And there was Speed Week on the Isle of Man, with German girls throwing kisses and flowers at me and my FLH. . . . You don't need to hear about that, except to note that European bikers did tip their helmets to the King of the Road.

Oh, the FLH had its downsides. The factory never did figure out how to keep the exhaust pipes attached to the heads, ditto for the plug from alternator to regulator. Nor could you say oil-tight and FLH in the same sentence without risking a longer nose. Worse, there were quality control problems in the early 1970s, mostly the result of making too many bikes too fast with too many new people on the line.

Meanwhile, the competition had been taking notes and it turned out it was easier for them to offer big machines with lots of extras than it was for Harley to invest in new, or even up-to-date, engines and suspensions and electrics.

When H-D did come up with a contemporary touring bike, the FLH became instant period piece. Then the factory took the old badge and put it on a new machine cloaked in old clothes, except they took away the sprung saddle. That change never sat right with me (chuckle).

But we needn't lose heart. The mass producers (read Japanese manufacturers) have taken all the places on the board. They've covered touring, commuting, sports and road racing, and dirt and dual sport.

But there's one niche they've never been able to fill, the one created by the FLH. Ten years after the real thing was replaced, collectors are still going after and appreciating the real thing. With fairing and boxes, it's now called a Bagger. With bare bars and rear fender, it's a Cruiser.

Either way, there's still nothing like the FLH on the road or the market. Even now, be you Dad or Junior, Mom or Sis, to spot that stout and gleaming profile, that vee packed with muscle and chrome, bearing a rider who's upright and relaxed and yes, aware of your awareness, is to repeat once again, "Golly! A motorcycle!"

Sidecars, or more properly termed combinations, are machines apart from the rest. They don't act like four-wheelers, and they sure don't act like bikes.

Chapter 17

1971 Super Glide

Survival of the Hippest

Super Glide took what owners were doing to their big twins and did it for them, by stripping extras like electric start and fitting the lighter front suspension and headlight from the XLCH. The result is lightness combined with muscle. Owner: Harley-Davidson Motor Company.

*Q*uote: "It will succeed in this country like no machine H-D has ever made or dreamed of making" (*Cycle* magazine, November 1970).

Fact: The 1971 FX, the original Super Glide, didn't sell all that well.

More important fact: The Super Glide was the baseline, the bedrock upon which Harley-Davidson built its own survival.

Once again, having said something positive and dramatic, we look at a dismal era. In the mid- and late-1960s, Harley-Davidson was in financial trouble and confusion and was taking it on the head and shoulders from rivals who had more models and a wider range. Harley's Italian imports couldn't keep up, the Sportster no longer was the fastest thing on the road, and the FLH, in becoming *the* touring machine, had equipped itself out of the rest of the markets.

Folks are funny creatures. When bikes came stripped, the owners piled on extras. When the factory supplied the extras, owners took them off. Chopped, as the saying became, or bobbed, when the fenders were trimmed back or a front fender went on the rear. Private or home or even backyard builders transformed the solid and square 74s into spare versions of motorcycle, bare bones, and stretched into the distance.

Willie G. Davidson, whose name is on the factory, was in charge of styling and was well aware of what people were doing with the product. He liked the theme. There were limits to what he had to work with, but the styling department took production parts, such as the FLH frame and rear suspension and engine and gearbox. They took the lightweight forks, 19in front wheel, and small headlight from the XLCH. They used a smaller version of the twin fuel tanks from the FLH, removed the electric starter and the huge battery needed to power it, and for the punchline, replaced the sprung tractor seat and fully valanced rear fender with a fiberglass seat and fender, quickly known as the Boatback.

No one item was terribly far out. All the parts were production, and even the fiberglass sections were shared; the boatback seat was a Sportster option that year.

The combination was beyond anything any factory had dared offer, to the extent that Willie G. and crew ran the photos up the flagpole, in one of the car magazines first and then in a survey on which the factory name did not appear. The motorcycle public was wild for the idea and styling and production got permission from management to put the model on the market.

No attempt was made to claim that the new model was anything other than what it was. The designation was FX, F for big twin engine, X from

141

Tanks and controls came from the FLH, while the red-white-and-blue Number One was Harley's answer to political diversions of the time.

As noted elsewhere, kick-start is grand when it works, disaster and disgrace when it doesn't. And never mind what the magazines say, sometimes the human leg doesn't get the job done.

142

the XL Sportster. The name was Super Glide, two words and no hyphen, for reasons nobody's ever given.

Boatback and tanks were done in white, with red and blue stripes and trim. This was an era in which both sides of several controversies drew heavily on patriotism. You could, as *Cycle* magazine noted, criticize or defend, say, the Vietnam War, and still wear red, white, and blue. Whichever way you viewed the world, the paint worked.

As did the overall look. The chunky rear tire and massive engine gave muscle and mass, the coiled power of a dragster or quarter horse. The spindly front was airy and graceful and the stepped seat and tapered taillight housing served as speedlines. The FX looked new, powerful, and fast.

As it was. As stated, the opening quote came from *Cycle*, which had a full test and cover story in the issue for November 1970. The date indicates the magazine was the first to test the

FX engine was stock FL series, the Shovelhead, with a smaller battery because start was kick only, and with both cylinders feeding one muffler. The device in front of the front exhaust pipe is the master cylinder and linkage for the rear brake. The new seating position moved the right peg so far forward there was no place else to put it.

Extended front end made the front leap forward, while the solid rear portion was crouched to spring. Patriotic paint didn't hurt, either.

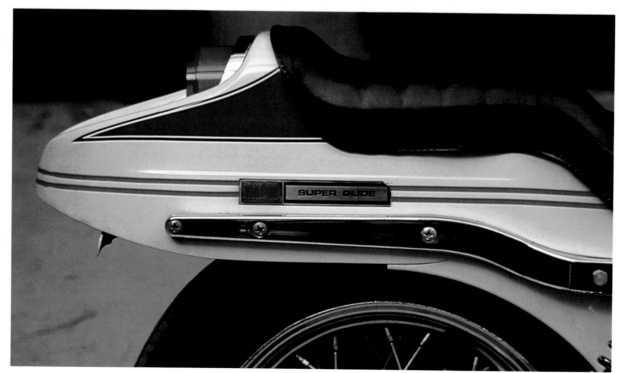

Boatback seat and fender came from the company's fiberglass plant. It was radical and got the public's attention but many buyers swapped for conventional components.

144

model. That in turn usually means that the mag that got the break will love the product.

Even so, the test seems fair today. The magazine explained where the FX came from. It looks like it handles, they said, and it does, and it looks fast, and it is, pity the tanks are too fat and the brakes aren't up to the job. Honest criticism, valid then and now.

In the facts column, the FX weighed 565lb with the 3.5gal tanks half full. That's 125lb less than a stock 1971 FLH and only 50 or 60lb more than the XL, which had grown to 1000cc by then. The FX wasn't as quick or nimble as the XL, but it performed with more show and less stress and anyway, there's at least as much to be gained by *looking* tough as there is by *being* tough.

Quoting *Cycle* again: "What does the bike do for you? How do you feel when you ride it? You feel like a damn king, is how you feel. . . . Everybody likes it; everybody has to like it. . . . It is terribly self-conscious, terribly extreme. It leaves itself no outs, brooks no compromises."

All true. Which makes the next part all the more interesting.

All the magazines felt pretty much the same way about the FX, one suspects in part because we and they do like outrageous statements and are glad to have something new to talk about.

The buying public wasn't quite as keen on the idea. Drawback number one was the boatback. One dealer recalls that he sold only two FXs with the stock seat and fender. The others in his consignment didn't move until he'd taken off the fiberglass and replaced it with a steel fender and either the tractor or an aftermarket seat. Willie G. had gone a bit too far, too fast. Or it may be that the design never did work on a motorcycle, never mind that now it's famous. For at least fifteen years after the boatback appeared, you could pick one up for a few bucks at any swap meet in the country. Right, as soon as they became scarce, the prices went up. Or was it vice versa? Either way, the originals are rarer and more popular now than they were then, which is one reason why the example shown is the one Willie G. saved in 1971 and is part of H-D's official collection.

Notes and names were still being taken. The 1972 FX came with steel rear fender and chopper-style dual seat. No more boatback. In 1973, the cumbersome and heavy-looking dual tanks were replaced by a smaller (3.5gal) single tank borrowed from the Italian-made single. And in 1974, the FX was joined by the FXE, that is, electric start became an option.

This makes sense. As noted elsewhere, kickstart is grand when it works, disaster and disgrace when it doesn't. And never mind what the magazines say, sometimes the human leg doesn't get the job done.

According to the factory records, in 1971 the factory sold 4,700 FXs, against 10,000 Sportsters and more than 6,500 FLs and FLHs. The FX went to 6,500 in 1972, minus the fiberglass, against 10,000 big twins and 17,000 XLs. The ratios were much the same in 1973. And in 1974, the plain FX sold half as many as did the FXE, 3,034 to 6,199.

What did this mean? *Cycle* was wrong, in the short term. The Super Glide didn't sell more than any other Harley in history. Nor did it hurt sales of the FLH or XLCH, which probably was better for the factory and the dealers.

There's a moral to the story, that the electric start gained sales, especially when 1974 was marginally less successful overall than 1973. As discussed, looking tough is enough when you also know the engine will fire in time for a stylish exit.

The long run is what matters here, though. The Super Glide went beyond just giving the dealer something new to sell. It got the public's attention, and it showed that Harley-Davidson could, and would, take chances and had faith in its own people and ideas.

Key here is that Willie G. and Company had given themselves a new platform, a better foundation on which to play the game they had to play, making better bricks with less straw, or chicken soup when there weren't any new chicken parts. They had a new cutting edge, a better parameter to stretch. The Low Rider, the Fat Bob, the Wide Glide, even the Super Glide II and FXRS Sport have all come from the FX. They had to come from the FX because they wouldn't have worked on either the touring bike or the paperboy bike.

So when we admire, lust after, or buy the Sturgis or Softail or Daytona, we do so only because Willie G. had some parts and some fiberglass and the guts to do something outrageous with them.

Chapter 18

1977 Low Rider

Another Stretch for the Envelope

Somewhere there's gotta be an axiom, some bit of folk wisdom about how it's best to keep the lead you've got.

Whatever that maxim is, it fits the Low Rider.

Motorcycle sales were booming in 1977. All the segments of the market were doing well, not least because the leading imports, as we said when we didn't wish to single out the Japanese, had begun upsizing, getting into the large sports and touring markets as well as motocross and tiddlers.

Harley-Davidson was benefiting only indirectly, if at all. AMF had rescued the company from dismemberment or insolvency (take your pick and write an angry letter if you don't agree), but AMF was much better at making capital investments than in improving the product. Plus, there was federal pressure on the emissions, noise, and safety fronts so what money there was for the product went in that direction.

Willie G. Davidson grins cheerfully now and says yes, the corporation didn't always understand the design staff back in the corporate days but that wasn't important because when it counted, they let him do what he believed had to be done.

In the case of the FXS Low Rider, he says, "We took the custom bubble and pushed it further."

The beginning was the FX/FXE Super Glide, introduced in 1971 and detailed in chapter 17. The first 'Glide was an instant hit and easily identified as both a mix of Big Twin and Sportster, and as the mass-produced heir to the custom/chopper style. The model sold well, and Willie and crew knew the Gang of Four wouldn't be far behind.

So they began with the Super Glide, the FL frame, the 74ci engine, and the XL front. They shortened the suspension so the seat height, at rest and with pre-load set at minimum, was a claimed 27in; for reference, *Cycle World* magazine checked with a tape measure and got 27.4in for the Low Rider and 31.9in for the 500cc Honda road bike introduced at the same time. The forks were set at a more rakish angle, which lowered the front and extended the wheelbase and moved the front wheel away from the engine, another chopper touch. The wheels were cast alloy, which added a modern, almost technical note. Wheels and basic panels were metallic gray, the only choice, while the barrels and heads got a black crackle finish, with polished highlights for the fins. Far as he knows, Willie G. did that first.

Low Rider took the Super Glide the next outrageous step. No more fiberglass but the suspension was lowered for the lowest seat height on the market. Owner: Lew Clark, Sacramento, California.

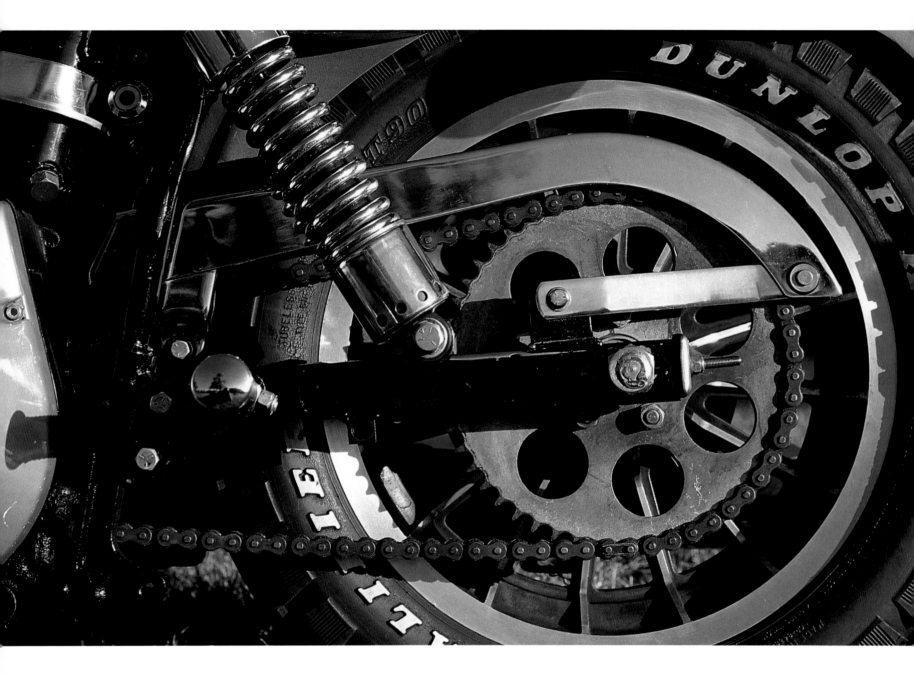

Low Rider frame was still FLH, with forward-mount shocks and attendant flexing of the swing arm. Cast wheels allowed use of tubeless tires.

The foot controls were moved forward a bit, the bars were lower and narrower than the previous Model FX as well as the average motorcycle, and the seat mimicked the king-and-queen style by being lower for the operator than the passenger.

Cycle World must have been staffed by novices at the time (okay, the staff was mostly new; I should know, being on the staff at the time). There was a fuss made over the use of two fuel tanks, 3.5gal total, known as Fat Bob tanks. They were from the days of bobbed motorcycles, trimmed and cut down. But with the big touring tanks, as in Fat.

What the kids hadn't realized was that the original FX came with those same tanks, right off the FLH, and then in 1973 changed to the single tank from the touring Italian-made H-D

Sprint. The logo on the twin tanks in 1977 was done in turn-of-the-century script and the medallions came from 1903 or so. But the brakes were disc, two in front and one in back, and although there was an electric leg as part of the package, care was taken to provide a kick lever, for emergencies and surely to give some heritage as well.

As the photos show, this was a neat, clean piece of work and of art.

There were some subtle prices to be paid. The lowered chassis and seat gave surer footing at lights and aided short people who wanted big bikes. But if you have to deal with, say, a 6in pothole and you've lowered the bike by shortening the rear suspension, you'll have less suspension travel to soak up the bump and that means you'll need stiff springs. Really stiff, which the Low Rider's were. Same goes in front, plus kicking the front wheel out from the frame gave a longer wheelbase; more stable on the straights, less eager to turn in town.

Now we come to what must be seen as a philosophical issue. The low and staggered seat and low, flat, and narrow handlebars were in perfect style. They gave the look of the traditional saddle tramp, arms straight, head tucked into the wind, back curved into that legendary million-mile slouch.

It's a wonderful way to look. It's not the all-time grandest way to spend your time on the highway or in town, though.

Forward controls and raised feet, the better to clear the ground from that lowered seat and suspension, made the gearshift a step-over proposition. Engine got black paint with polished fins and electric start was now mandatory.

Forks for FX and the XL series were stronger than they'd been and thanks to the double disc brakes, stopping power matched the big engine.

The magazine writers found themselves liking the big beast. It was a thinking man's chopper, said one report, the look of one man's good taste, and the public will like it.

Low Rider went back to the twin tanks of the first FX after a flirtation with the single tank off Harley's Italian models. Still one muffler, but with more sweep to the pipes.

Willie G. had tapped a nerve. The Low Rider gave exactly the look it was supposed to give. It had style.

Style rules the world. Nobody minds that most of the time, except in this particular case, the function of the machine had been hampered a bit so the rider would look good. At one time, when the look was invented, there were reasons for having twin fuel tanks, and the seat could only be low because there wasn't any rear suspension except for the seat itself. But the new machine made to the old design wasn't as good as it could have been.

For what could have been another handicap, the motorcycle magazines in 1977 knew that Harley-Davidson was coming out of a bad patch. They wanted to do what they could to help ... but only where and when it didn't compromise journalistic standards.

So the big books tested the Harleys, something that hadn't been done several years earlier when the scribes all fawned over motorcycles from east of the Americas.

The testers were willing to learn. They knew the FXS was basically sound; after all, it had an engine that had, shall we say, stood the test of time. They liked the efficiency of the big engine under little stress. They didn't like the ponderous steering and the effort required to work the clutch and brakes and gearshift. They made justified fun of having to fill the left tank, then the right tank because if you didn't, fuel would flow from the higher right side out the filler if you took off the left cap: One can imagine the expert tester's rage when he did this in public.

They weren't exactly sure why, but they found themselves liking the big beast. It was a thinking man's chopper, said one report, the look of one man's good taste, and the public will like it.

Exactly right. The Low Rider was introduced in 1977 as a late model for that year and it sold out. In model year 1978, with production ready in time, the Low Rider outsold the regular Super Glide and the FLH and everything in the line except the basic Sportster, the loss leader of the day. No Harley-Davidson ever achieved more, at a more important time, with so little spent on parts.

In the case of the FXS Low Rider's design, Willie G. says, "We took the custom bubble and pushed it further."

Chapter 19

1977 XLCR

Putting the Answer Before the Question

When Willie G. Davidson makes a mistake, it's a beaut. Yes, that's a play on words and a judgment call all at the same time.

The XLCR began in the 1960s, when owners of sports bikes began modifying their street rides to look and act as much like road racers as the law allowed. The forces behind this sprang up first and foremost in England, followed in the United States by guys who favored (for the most part) road racing versus flat track, and British equipment rather than American or Japanese. There was a market here, though, and the magazines paid attention to the work being done, especially when it happened that the crowd riding these bikes liked to zoom from hangout to hangout. Thus the modified machines and riders became known as Cafe Racers.

Willie G. is an artist and trained designer and is always open to new ideas. He rides and reads and travels and knew about the new fashion.

At the same time, the Sportster was languishing a bit. By the mid-1970s, the rivals from east of the United States (known as Westerners) had faded away but the competition to the west (whom we call Easterners) had come on strong and yanked (sorry) the sports bike market away from Harley.

The Sportster had a following and the XLCH could still hold its own in class, but overall the design was out of date well before retro styling came into being.

Willie G. had strung together a line of hits, as we've just seen. So he did some design and some parts selection and got the backing to have the engineering staff improve the machine itself. Then, early in 1977 the company announced and introduced the limited-production (as in Get One Before They're Gone) XLCR—no prize for guessing what CR stood for.

The changes were basically improvements. First, the actual frame. The older XL used a casting at the upper rear of the engine cradle, to hold the seat mount and the tops of the rear shock absorbers and the oil tank and battery. It was a wide, cramped package and because the shocks were so far forward, their lower ends attached to the middle of the swing arm legs. The hub and axle were at the end of the swing arm, of course, and it isn't difficult to imagine the bending and twisting forces and the leverage exerted on the arm when the input was at one end and the resistance was in the middle. Nor was the actual swing arm all that sturdy.

The new frame copied that of the XR-750, with steel tubing to form the junction, and with tubes extended rearward so the shocks were

XLCR had a road racer profile in front and an aft section based on the dirt track XR-750. Owner: Mike Shattuck, Sacramento, California.

Quarter fairing gave some wind protection at speed, especially with the rider moved back on the bike in road-race style.

vertical and directly atop the rear hub. The swing arm was boxed, just to give extra heft. As a nice addition, the longer full frame cleared more space for the oil tank and battery, narrowing the components beneath the seat.

The engine was the basic 1000cc XL unit, with black barrels and covers and so forth. It had a distinctive exhaust system that joined the front and rear pipes at the center of the engine's vee, then routed the rear pipes aft on the right and the left pipe around the front of the engine and back, all in matte black paint.

Wheels were cast alloy from Morris, a supplier to the road racers at the time, and the brakes were Kelsey-Hayes discs, two in front and one in back. Going along with the road race theme was a tiny front fender, rearset footpegs,

low bars, and a tiny fairing, with smoked glass. The seat, with room for one and only one person, blended into the rear fender, which looked like an extended version of the XR-750 unit with taillight tucked below the panel and the license plate below that. The fuel tank was a full 4gal in capacity, the largest tank ever fitted to a Sportster by the factory and a welcome change from the silly little 2.2gal tank on the conventional XLH.

In sum, the XLCR hit the showrooms as a normal sort of Harley variation, with paint and panels and mechanical bits juggled some and swapped some, in hope of giving more character at not much expense.

In the strict mechanical transportation sense, the XLCR worked fine. Stock gearing was

a tooth lower than the plain 1977 XL used and power and weight were about the same, so the CR did well in the tests.

In what might truly have been a happy accident, the CR was in some ways a better daily driver than the plain XL. The stock number was pushed in the chopper direction, with high bars and forward, upright seating, and a seat that didn't match its soft parts with the soft places of the rider.

The Cafe Racer had lower bars and a seat moved aft. The rearset pegs were a better match for the other locations so the posture, aided by the little fairing, worked on the highway. The homebuilt cafe racers made from standard road bikes usually made physical demands that limited their appeal and function, other than racing between cafes. But the Harley Cafe Racer gave away less function in behalf of form than did the XL.

So after all that, after all the research into fashion and the engineering and investments and the persuasion of management that this was the time and place . . . the CR didn't sell nearly as well as hoped or expected. The factory produced about 2,000 examples in model year 1977, another 1,200 or so in 1978, and that was that.

Except for the dealers who'd been convinced and stocked up. Arlen Ness bought twenty-two CRs in one swoop from a Texas dealer who

The frame was similar to the standard XLH from steering head back to seat mount, but the XLCR frame rails extended back to above the rear axle, as the XR-750 frame did. So the CR's shock absorbers were above the axle and the swing arm didn't flex as much. Two years later all the XLs got this improvement.

Willie G. used just about all the black he could get. The exhaust pipes, even, were matte black. They joined below the air cleaner, then one pipe ran back on the right and the other went forward, under and around the frame and back on the left.

ordered fifty at a time. Ness wasn't that keen on the model, he says now, but the CR was prime raw material and he got a bargain.

As I've said before, failure is an orphan. But this failure has several components, if not villains.

One was timing. The model was announced and introduced on schedule but deliveries weren't, and as any marketer knows, not having supply when you've generated demand hurts.

It might also have hurt that the CR came only as a solo, with no original provision for carrying a passenger. Posturing aside, the guy buying a bike on which he can't take his near-

and-dear is giving himself an extra handicap in what often turns into a contest. (In fairness, the factory offered a two-up seat as an option in 1978, better late than never, as your mom said.)

One could even make a case against all the black paint. The color is classic and still makes a fashion statement, or so some people believe. Black still does well in the custom and chopped modes, and on MTV.

But in the middle and late 1970s, motocross and popularity had persuaded the road racing crowd to deck riders and bikes in bright colors— Honda Red, Yamaha Yellow, Harley Orange, and Kawasaki Green.

Black chrome was used for the air cleaner, the oval style known around the dealerships as the Ham Can.

Instruments were tucked inside the fairing, where the crouched rider could see them and know just how much trouble he was about to get into.

The true flaw, or so I have deduced from a distance, was that the cafe crowd didn't want Harleys, and the Harley-Davidson chaps had no interest in road racing, real or imagined: The factory team had dropped out of national and world road racing several years before this, with no loss in sales.

Willie G. wasn't completely wrong, though. The CR did appeal to collectors with an eye for style and rarity, and it did appeal to enthusiasts who could see beyond the either-or mentality. The CR became known as, well, I hate to say an investment. Call it instant cult object. Within a year or two so many people knew the price would go up, that it never went down.

"Maybe we were too slow in producing them," Willie G. says now, and "Maybe the timing was wrong."

He's made up for it by now. But Mike Shattuck, owner of a Sacramento H-D dealership and an H-D employee when the CR was new, says, "The Cafe Racer broke Willie's heart." Shattuck also owns the CR pictured here.

Chapter 20

1980 FLT Tour Glide

The Wind
Beneath the Eagle's Wings

Radical probably isn't the first word one would associate with the FLT at a glance, not with words like traditional, conventional, solid, and big in the neighborhood.

But radical is the word that works best.

For this we can thank a mix of practicality and politics.

In the late 1970s Harley-Davidson was in trouble. The motorcycle company was a subsidiary of AMF (American Machine and Foundry), a conglomerate. The parent company had invested money in the division, one could argue that it kept H-D alive, but the money had been spent for capital projects and not on the product. As a result, the product line was out of date, so was the technology, and perhaps even worse, there was a perception in the biker world that nothing interesting ever happened in Milwaukee.

There were able and intelligent people at H-D and AMF, and they managed to wrangle money for research and development. They knew where the market was and what their products needed, and decided that the best place to make the most from what they had, was in the touring sector.

The project was an up-to-date touring machine, a dresser, a new top for the line, and a replacement for the venerable FLH. They didn't have a free hand, however, as the new machine would have to use the 80ci version of the even-more-venerable FL engine.

The secret of the project was an engine mounting system. It used what we can call shock absorbers. By having links and pivots and stops, the insulators could let the big twin rock and vibrate as before—except that the vibrations didn't get to the frame or the occupants. The idea wasn't unique, but it worked and still works. Occupant comfort was enhanced. Just as useful if less obvious, not having the cycle parts shaken meant they weren't as likely to fatigue or fall off and that meant less maintenance and repair, real or imagined.

The mounting system (as well as advances in design) called for a new frame. The FLT frame was much stiffer than the FLH frame, didn't use iron, and was designed from the onset to carry full luggage and weather gear, such as saddlebags and a fairing. The package was designed as a system so it went together easily and didn't need to be adapted.

Because there was a new frame, the front and rear suspension could be given more wheel travel and thus control, and the engine could be raised to give more clearance and that meant the bike could lean farther, more safely. The new frame allowed something, well, radical in that the fork tubes were mounted behind the steering

The FLT was as large as it looks here, and came with all the extras, as in full fairing, saddlebags, top box, and case guards that the touring rider would expect. Owner: Harley-Davidson Motor Co.

Sturdy front fork tubes and valenced fender are typical touring Harley, with disc brake and cast wheel adding modern touches.

stem instead of in front: Without getting into deep gearhead jargon, by swapping tubes and stem and using different angles and not having tubes and stem parallel, the FLT engineers provided stable and light steering for what was a really big machine.

The engine got the latest in oil control, as in valve seals and a spin-on oil filter, a new and quieter exhaust system, and an electronic ignition with programmed, as opposed to mechanical, spark advance.

The separate gearbox housed five speeds forward, with the ratios a few teeth closer together than the old four-speed's spread, and final drive was taller, so the engine revved slower and easier on the highway. In what was later seen as

an interim step, the final-drive chain was enclosed, so it ran in oil and not grit. This protected the chain, increased chain life, cleaned up the traditional mess, and gave the owners something to talk about when the BMW and Gold Wing guys bragged about shaft drive.

The FLT's permanent, part-of-the-package fairing mounted on the frame. It was big and efficient and carried two car-size headlights. There were stowage bins in the fairing, and the side and top boxes were also included in the basic model, so there were plenty of places to pack stuff. The new frame didn't have room for the old sprung seat post, but there was an optional sprung seat. Most buyers opted for the solidly mounted dual seat because it was lower.

Floorboards for the driver, with rocker shift lever so you push down for both up and down shifts. Rare for a Harley big twin, the front cylinder's exhaust pipe tucks inside the frame in front and then routes down the left side to its own muffler.

Fairing was mounted on the frame—as opposed to the FLH fairing, on the fork tubes and clamps—where side winds wouldn't disturb the steering.

The FLT arrived as a properly planned stepup, and it worked well on several fronts. First, people bought them. There was a market for a new and improved touring bike, just as the planners had counted on.

Next and no less important, the critics, aka the motorcycle press, were impressed. This might have been partially because there were new reporters, who hadn't gone through the Yank versus Brit exchanges of previous years and thus didn't have anything against H & D. It might have been because the magazines by then were staffed by people who'd been subjected to journalism training and were prepared to be fair—and harsh, when justified.

It might have been that the FLT was a good touring machine.

In any case, and my vote goes for explanation three, mitigated by one and two, the reports were favorable. The FLT Tour Glide got good marks in the normal tests and even held its own in group and comparison tests, a venue to which Harleys hadn't been invited for years.

161

Shovelhead engine was expanded to 80ci, and mounted in rubber—well, some sort of flexible and absorbent material—to isolate the riders from the vibration.

All the improvements were, well, improvements. The Shovelhead was long in the tooth by then, but there was enough power and the engine and gearbox stayed cleaner longer. The new model was marginally slower than the old one but that was because of all the extras, so it didn't matter.

What mattered to the buyer was that the FLT was big but it steered like a lighter bike, it

had the big twin but didn't shake like the older models, and so forth.

The FLT put Harley-Davidson back into the demonstration business. The make's reputation had suffered to the point that people didn't believe all the improvements, or so H-D management believed, so they sent out a fleet of demo FLTs to the various rallies held by the touring folk and let the skeptics ride the FLTs. Many

162

bought and the others at least went home impressed and told their friends.

There were major benefits beyond the actual sales. Within the next of the concentric circles that comprise the motorcycling world, there are people who are enthusiasts. They may not buy a new scooter every year, but they pay attention. With the FLT, Harley-Davidson had a valid claim to engineering and technical advancement. The firm's reputation was greatly improved by the new perceptions, which may have mattered as much as the tangible results in sales and dollars.

This is because in 1981 some of the execs from within Harley, and some who'd arrived with AMF, put all they had in hock and then pledged everything but their firstborn to the banks, and bought Harley-Davidson back from AMF, made it a separate company again. They got help on the loans by selling stock, going public as the company had done earlier.

This sounds cynical, but the average investor buys because he or she hears good things about a given stock from other people. The financial pages were looking for heroes and the guys at Harley filled the bill, so the stock issue sold well and went up in price, making the stock a better deal for all.

The original FLT wasn't the complete package; there were improvements on the way, like the Evolution engine and belt drives and so forth. They'd been in the works when bad ol' AMF held the reins, to be fair here.

But the FXRs, the belts, and new engines for the FL, FX, and XL series, the frames and suspension, and all the keen new bits, arrived after the eagle was once again flying alone, as the public relations campaign put it when the company was bought back.

The FLT wasn't just a product, or even a good product.

It was a good product when that was the only thing that could have kept Harley-Davidson in business.

Raised passenger seat lets the occupant see over the operator, while leaning on a backrest in turn braced by the top box. Nobody's going to fall off the back, the passenger's traditional fret.

163

Chapter 21

1984 FXST Softail

The Old Looks New and the New Looks Old

The Softail, and we must pause here to insert the circle R trademark that H&D insists on, is such a milestone it should appear in this book twice, once for its great leap forward, and again for its successful exploitation of the past.

Make that three times. This has to be Willie G.'s finest hour.

Harley-Davidson's new-from-old era begins just after a group of Harley execs took matters into their own hands and bought H-D from its corporate owners. They did it on faith and piles of borrowed money and nobody knew better than they did that the product needed improvement.

The engineering department got hold of all the claims and records and warranty work for the big twin, the F series engine that came directly from the Knucklehead 61 of 1936, and figured out just how much trouble the Shovelhead—the version introduced in 1966—was. It was a lot. And while there had been some still-secret work done by outsiders on a really new and different engine, there wasn't money now to do more than revise the old one.

So that's what they did. The iron cylinders were replaced with barrels made of aluminum alloy. The hemispherical combustion chambers of the Shovelhead were changed to side-squish chambers. The domed pistons were given a flat crown. There were stronger connecting rods, a more efficient system to drain the oil from the heads, and a new electronic ignition with the advance curve controlled by vacuum (throttle opening in the working world) as well as engine speed.

None of the improvements were new in the sense of radical, as *Cycle World* noted, but they were new to Harley-Davidson. The changes cured most of the ailments that had plagued the old engine, and allowed a higher compression ratio, resulting in more efficient power and higher revs. The V2 Evolution engine, as H-D named it at the introduction, had 10 percent more power, 15 percent more torque, and weighed 20lb less than the iron-barrel Shovelhead.

(As sort of a late addition to history, the *Cycle World* story nicknamed the revised engine the Blockhead, a name picked by writer Steve Kimball because he wanted to see if it would stick. The indulgent then-editor, me, let him get away with it and sure enough, the nickname stuck. Or that's how I remember it now.)

This portion of Harley history is the part that appears in books about how to get an ailing company back on its feet. For good reason, because the revised engine was surely the best solution for the greatest number, at the lowest cost, in the annals of The Motor Company.

Another Harley-Davidson trademark is the ability to build motorcycles for the people who buy them: When the market decided that new bikes that look like restorations were the thing, H-D presented the Softail. Owner: Carolyn Jensen, Sacramento, California.

That's the technical part, how the old became new.

Another era for H-D began at a Harley-Davidson rally, where H-D chairman Vaughn Beals noticed something really different. That, in itself, is worth noting because Beals was an AMF guy, an industrial executive who was assigned to H-D and became intrigued enough to put his career and his bank balance into the buy-out.

What Beals saw was a suspension design by Bill Davis, an independent engineer who had redone the swing arm and frame and shocks of his own bike. The suspension was hidden beneath the gearbox, and the parts that showed looked like the frame rails from the old rigid-rear bikes.

Future generations may have trouble accepting this, but when Harley-Davidson began to return to life, the rest of the world had fallen in love with modern versions of the past. Retro-style, as they said, was in fashion, so when the

Timer—if we can still use that term—for the electronic ignition is behind the cover for the camshaft and alternator.

Bike's owner has fitted factory-approved chrome to the front axle covers, fork boots, timer cover, footrests, chain guard, derby (clutch) cover, starter solenoid and end cap, oil filter, gas caps, and handlebar clamp.

Central console for the speedometer and warning lights came from earlier models. The raised eagle on the cap was added by the owner.

Easy to see why the handlebars are called Buckhorns, and the fork tubes and mounts earned the title Wide Glide.

other guys in your crowd had new Harleys, the way to stand out was to have an old one.

Or a new one, with, for instance, the modern electrics and performance and oil-tight reliability of the V2 engine, but blended in with the looks of the older bikes.

Click, the lightbulbs went on above H-D's collective head.

All departments sat down to design this model, which would use the new engine, of course, but would have the old-style four-speed gearbox instead of the five-speed in the other FX models. And the V2 would mount solidly in the frame, while the others used the engine mount, introduced in 1980, that isolated the engine and its vibrations from the occupants.

You see the part about difficult to understand: The Softail, so called because there was more rear suspension than could be seen, had less wheel travel than the other FX models. It had more vibration coming through to the rider and passenger, and the engine revved more and

167

made more noise and (presumably) wore faster than did the same unit in the more reasonable chassis. In keeping with the theme of the bike, the seating and controls were placed so the occupants looked like Hollywood's version of the open road. So at the same time they weren't as comfortable as they would have been if the controls had been placed for riding.

Having said all that, one scarcely need add that the Softail was the hit of the model year. Yet all the magazines explained once again, just as they had when the Big Four from across the pond began imitating choppers, that this wasn't the way to build motorcycles.

And it may not have been.

What it was, was a way to *sell* motorcycles.

This isn't merely cynicism on the part of the press. The late Charley Thompson, a motorcycle fan who worked his way up to president of H-D, used to say that the dealer's biggest job was finding things for his customers to do with their machines once they'd bought them.

The Softail was the perfect motorcycle for the people who bought one. Yes, you could explain (as I have done countless times) that the seating position and the location of the pegs and the angle one's head sits in the wind are all wrong for riding coast to coast. The Softail owner nods and says, yeah but see, what I do is ride down to the cafe on Sunday and then maybe we go to the park and once a year or so the wife and I take a weekend ride. When I go to the other coast, the happy owner says, I call American Airlines even though their seats aren't much more comfortable.

This is perfectly fair. Nobody in the developed world needs a motorcycle, not in the sense of transportation at low cost and least space. Motorcycling is a sport and if one rider likes to style instead of scorch, it's a free country.

And it's a free market (to a degree anyway). The Softail was a tremendous success in that market. Better for H&D, the Softail was a high-ticket item: In our next installment we'll look at an equally good approach at the other end of the new bike market. Every Softail sold made money for the factory and the dealer.

One more point. At home, Mark Twain used words most of us learned in the Navy. His wife meant to shame him by repeating the offense, but he just looked at her and said, "My dear, you've learned the words but you can't carry the tune."

Previous page
Evolution engine is a completely modern top, as in cylinder heads and valve gear, carried on much-improved cases and flywheels.

Rear frame section and oil tank below seat are close copies of rigid-rear ancestors, while hidden below the engine and gearbox are shocks and springs.

Non-riders always find this hard to believe, but you can control the throttle, the front brake and the turn signal with one hand, at once, while both feet and your left hand are also engaged.

So it was with the Softail and its rivals. The bigger companies did their best. They tacked odd shapes of chrome in places Harleys have chrome, they stretched here and stubbed there. It never worked. The big twins from the Big Four have always been obvious imitations, and anybody who can't see it deserves to buy one.

If there's ever been a motorcycle only Harley-Davidson could have built, it has to be the Softail.

Chapter 22

XR-750

Ruler of the Roost

When the XR-750 was born the first time, things looked bad. And then, they got worse.

Late in the 1960s, the British contingent in the AMA overturned the 750cc side-valve, 500cc overhead-valve equivalency formula that had worked since the 1930s. The Brits did it because they had a selection of singles and twins, modern by the standards of the day, that could easily have become the production racers contesting for the national title.

Harley-Davidson was caught with its plans down. The official factory racer was the old KR, still competitive but ten years (at least) out of date.

Team manager Dick O'Brien did the only thing he could do: He took the iron engine from the club-race version of the Sportster, reduced the stroke to meet the displacement limit, and stuffed the makeshift engine into the KR's frame. The result, named the XR-750 because it was the Racing version of the X series engine, was overweight and underpowered and fragile. The engines blew up and the bikes broke down. The factory made 200 examples, as the rules required. Word got out, half the bikes were sold and the rest scrapped or dismantled for parts, and Triumph and BSA won the national championships in 1970 and 1971.

Dismal is the word that works here.

But if the factory had been caught out, O'Brien had been biding his time. He'd known the side-valve couldn't go on forever. The iron engine had been a way to fly the flag and keep the shop warm: Naturally, the racing problems came during the financial and industrial relations conflicts that arose during the AMF takeover or rescue (choose one, depending on your bias), so there wasn't enough money to do it right the first time.

But in 1972, the XR-750 was born again. It won right out of the box and twenty years later it's still winning. Meanwhile Triumph, BSA, Norton, and the other English bikes are gone, Yamaha has been run out of the park twice, and the only make that's been able to compete with the XR-750 has been Honda, who did it the old-fashioned way—by a higher dollar and higher tech version of the Harley.

Amazing. Especially when an educated glance at the XR engine shows that it's normal H and D practice, an adaptation of what the factory already had.

In detail, the XR engine is descended from the XL, with the 45deg vee, the four single cams in an arc in the timing case, the built-up crankshaft and chain primary and gearbox stuffed into a cavity that's part of the engine cases.

Learn to slide the rear wheel under full power out of a turn while steering with your body weight 'cause the front tire is off the ground, and you'll be riding like Scotty Parker, winner of four-straight national championships. Legal owner: Harley-Davidson Motor Co.; real owner: Bill Werner.

The XR is a deceptively simple design. Every specification on the bike—wheelbase, ride heights, steering rake angle, and so forth—is used for tuning to the track, and every spec is widely variable. At one end of the spectrum you can see the ancestral KR and XL, at the other is an engine Honda took home and copied.

The XR engine is vastly more different than it first appears. With bore of 3.125 and stroke of 2.98in, it's the only Harley on which the bore exceeds the stroke, or oversquare as they say. The engine cases are cast in a more durable and stronger (and more expensive to make and machine) alloy than the XL. The main bearings are self-aligning ball bearings, for less friction and longer life under higher stress, and the massively finned cylinders and heads are unique to

the racing engine, as are the choices of camshafts, the pair of giant Mikuni carbs, the tuned exhaust and boom-box muffler high on the left, and the electronic, self-generating, dual-plug firing one-cylinder-at-a-time ignition.

The XR-750 is unique even to racing, in that by 1992 the 1972 production racing machine had become a multiple-choice kit bike.

The 1972 rules called for 200 examples to be built and offered for sale, with all parts available

to anybody who had the money. Harley-Davidson met the rules, of course. But AMA racing is the venue of only a few hundred riders and teams, each of whom wants an advantage and most of whom like to do things his or her way.

So, the first XR-750s came in batches of 200, then 100-plus, then 100, and that tapered off to when demand warranted, which has since become . . . a parts book and advice. The latest, improved version of the XR engine came during a production run in 1991, with new cylinder heads and stronger lower end. The engines, in the sense of cases, heads, barrels and cranks, and so forth, are in stock at the factory: The racing team has nearly 100 suppliers of parts, and only a few hundred customers—AMA flat-track pros buying through their local dealerships.

Due to historical accident, for instance the invention of motocross and the decline in the number of flat-track locations and riders, and the specialized nature of the racing itself, it became foolish for any of the factories to pretend that the buyer was racing a stock bike. The rules were relaxed and the factories were required to certify engines, while frames, tanks, suspension, wheels, and the rest were free choice. Because outsiders could make and distribute such parts more quickly and easily than the factories could, the Harley racing department now gets the team's parts off the shelf some of the time, and the frames and suspension and tanks, for instance, from outside sources. You can't buy an XR frame from the factory anymore, but they'll be happy to sell you cases and ignition and tell you where the other stuff comes from.

That's the first half of the kit. Here's where the multiple-choice part comes in. Each tuner, skilled scientist, or mechanic who prepares the

The very latest version of a design that dates back, in general, to the XL of 1957. Still 45 degrees, ohv, unit construction, dry clutch, four speeds forward, and so forth, the 1992 XR-750 cranks out 100bhp or you don't bother driving to the track 'cause you won't be in the hunt. Two carburetors feed from the engine's right rear; the dual ignition is the polished circle at the engine's lower right; and the two-stage oil pump is at the bottom center of the crankcases. Because the rider needs space to plant his left boot on the track, gearshift and rear brake levers are both on the right.

Lovely piece of machine work mounts the clutch release arm (the vertical piece in the center), the right peg, and the master cylinder for the rear brake. As with boats, you save space and weight if one part can serve several purposes.

Art and magic is what we have here. The XR-750 is sharp and specialized and clean, all machine and nothing there that needn't be there.

bike for each track, can and does adjust every part on the machine for the specific track and weather. Cams and carbs and exhaust pipes are swapped, compression ratio is varied, gears and tires and wheelbase and even the height of the swing arm pivot are moved and relocated and massaged into exactly the combination that rider and team think or guess will work on that occasion. So on the one hand, all XR-750s are the same, and on the other hand, no two are alike and the race is run to see who's done it best.

During the past few seasons, the guys who've done it best are tuner Bill Werner and rider Scott Parker, operators of the XR shown here.

The facts are flexible, but the rules require a minimum weight of 315lb, and that's what this bike weighs with empty tanks. Wheelbase will be close to the 57in used when the model appeared and while the output varies with state of tune, a good normal XR-750 will have 100bhp fresh from the engine dynamometer.

The team let ESPN mount a camera (upper right, under tape) on the rear fender to broadcast the Pomona race. The lens faced the riders behind Parker.

Factory team rider Kevin Atherton, top tuner/winningest mechanic/team mainstay Bill Werner, and national champ Scott Parker (l-r), are not all that happy about lap times in practice.

Next page

Scott Parker in action, on the Pomona, California, half mile in 1991. The number one plate signifies he's the defending champion, a title he successfully defended that year. The plate is blue and yellow because those are the colors of Camel, sponsor of the series.

There's more magic involved than science, though. The frame, from Terry Knight according to Werner's specs, is full cradle, made of mild steel tubing. Note the dual rear shocks and telescopic forks; the main machine for this race ran giant conventional forks and the back-up bike was fitted with male-slider forks. Both come from motocross. No radical thinking, not much unobtanium. Werner and his peers say their adjustable flexible fliers work better than the space-age monoshock monocoques seen in road racing, so that's what they use.

Art and magic is what we have here. The XR-750 is sharp and specialized and clean, all machine and nothing there that needn't be there. To see and hear these crisp little monsters barrel into a turn at 100mph is to know their riders are doing something you and I can't possibly do, and nothing has ever done it better than the XR-750.

From the left, the XR engine's line of descent is unmistakable. Length of exhaust pipe from port to collector is critical, which is why the careful curves. Plunger device outboard of the front head is a steering damper, to calm the front wheel if it begins to shake.

Chapter 23

Evolution XLH

Little Brother Saves the Day

Evolution Sportster has proven to be a prime factor in getting new prospects into the showroom and onto Harleys. Owner: Steve Kimball, El Toro, California.

One of Harley lore's more obscure rules is that big twin guys like to mock the Sportster. Why, I've never been able to fathom, but it's been that way ever since the invention of the big and little bikes.

It's fun. There's a gal who's barely five feet tall and has a sidecar on her FLH, the full-dress version because she's not tall enough to hold the machine up at stop lights. Suggest an XL and she draws herself to full height and objects, "Sportsters are dirt bikes."

They're also known as baby bikes and girls' bikes. The best joke comes from Arlen Ness, who can make fun because he has owned a flock of XLCRs and thus doesn't mean the jibe, is that the Sportster is the paperboy bike.

Fun, but not fair. We've seen the Sportster figuratively invent the Superbike, the rortin' snortin' bad boy's ride. We've seen the XLCR redefine style, even if it didn't sell.

In 1986 we saw the Sportster open a new chapter in Harley-Davidson's saga of survival.

The XLH's chapter begins in 1983, when the newly independent Motor Company was clawing itself out of the red, doing more with less. They had the XL engine, which basically dated back to 1972, or 1956, or even to 1952 if you want to discard details.

By sort of backward good luck, the Big Four had run into inflation; the Japanese yen was strong or the dollar was weak but either way, the price of a Japanese motorcycle had gone up.

H-D took careful advantage. The company introduced the XLX, a Sportster with the small tank, solo seat, basic black paint, and a sticker price of $3,995. The model was a loss leader, as they say in the retail trades. The dealer made a modest profit but the factory probably didn't, even though the production line equipment had been paid off years ago.

What really mattered was that people who'd always assumed the Japanese bikes were cheaper and the Harleys were priced out of reach could suddenly read the papers and learn that the XLX was something they could afford. So they dropped in on the H-D dealership and, assuming the dealer had some savvy, were made welcome and bought their first Harley, which was the whole idea all along.

But the actual machine was woefully out of date. It was overweight and overcomplicated and not all that reliable, sorry to say.

The engineering department had been as busy as the sales staff. Model year 1986 brought the XLH-883, in the Harley manner a mix of new and old.

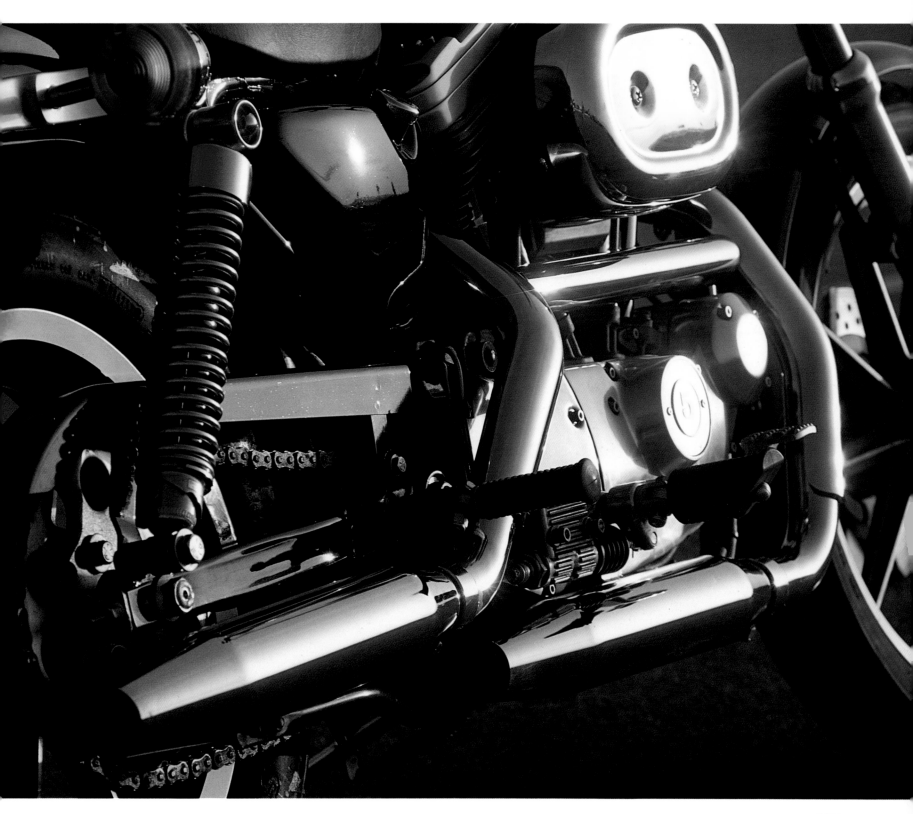

The old was easy. It was the basic approach, the stripper machine, the intro model, with plain paint and tiny tank and solo seat . . . and a price tag reading $3,995.

But the engine was virtually new. The label read 883 because the bore and stroke were 3.0x3.8in, same as the original XL back in 1957, and with same displacement of 883cc.

The outline was traditional, as the designers changed the profile as little as they could. There was the 45deg vee, the four one-lobe cams, and so forth.

But the cylinders and heads were aluminum, not iron. And the valve sizes and ports, the shape of the combustion chamber, and location of the spark plug, all the important bits, were new and improved and based on the Evolution version of the big twin.

The factory calculated that the old iron XL engine had 455 parts, including fasteners. The alloy XL engine had 426 parts, 29 fewer, and 206 of them were new.

For the next step, the new parts and design worked. The engine was lighter and smaller and

Staggered dual exhaust pipes meet noise rules by the unsightly addition of a balance tube below the air cleaner. Frame has been redone, with no more cast iron junctions and with much less flex.

As we'd expect, the Evo XL has alloy heads and cylinders and a completely new combustion chamber, all for more power and cleaner running. But the engine surely looks like the earlier ones and they still put the ignition switch and choke knob down inboard of the rider's left knee.

simpler, and more efficient since it got the same power from the more basic package, and it would last longer at the same output because there was less stress. Clutch pull was reduced, shifting effort was simplified, and so forth all the way down the line.

The new engine naturally gave new life to the Sportster line. It did the best work in the same place as the original loss leader, the XLX.

The new engine went into the XLH-883, with black paint, low bars, solo seat, tiny tank, one front disc brake, and a speedometer as the

Sporting aspect has been retained by keeping the small fuel tank from the XLCH, which in turn borrowed it from the racers. Dual seat is an option.

lone instrument. Same basic package, same $3,995 tag on the bars.

The difference mostly was that there were those who'd looked with some skepticism at the XLX. Sure, the price was right. But the engine was old and the improvements the new owners had managed to make didn't fix all the flaws.

The new engine changed that instantly. As any sales rep will admit, there's more than one way to lure the buyer into the showroom. Price is one, fashion is another, newness is a third.

What the Evolution Sportster did was add "new and improved" to the basic appeal of a good price. Ever since the introduction of the V2 big twin, with big new price tags to match, there had been potential buyers who wanted a new Harley but couldn't justify the new ones and weren't quite sold on the old ones. . . . Yup, I speak for myself here.

When the Evo XL arrived, there was no excuse left, or perhaps the excuse not to buy had become the excuse to whip down to the credit union and get into more trouble. Which is just what I, and all the others who bought new XLs, did. By the tens of thousands.

The next step was the 1100cc XL engine, a mildly bored out version of the 883, for a lot more money. This has become virtually a science at Harley-Davidson. The 1100 was replaced by a 1200, yes the same size as the big twin used to be, and there came a five-speed gearbox along with the four-speed, and a belt final drive to replace the chain at last, and an optional bigger tank. And there were the usual higher bars, a tachometer, a dual seat and saddlebags, and special paint, all the options Harley-Davidson (and Ford and Honda and everybody else) has come up with over the years. We tell ourselves we just want to talk about the stripper, and they let us talk ourselves into all the extras, and why not?

As writer Nora Ephron said about a subject entirely different, how can you hate somebody who's got your number?

Next in the list of benefits was this: the new XL was a motorcycle that the company could build more efficiently. Harley-Davidson was learning from the Japanese and worked out ways to reduce costs; for instance, the less time a frame spends in the warehouse, the less time between when you pay the supplier and the dealer pays you back. The XLH reduced costs as well as parts, so when it was sold at the low price,

Previous page
Nothing like a fore-and-aft twin for narrowness. Ham Can air cleaner, on the left here, does intrude on the rider's knee room.

Cast wheels are now standard wear on the basic XLH, with spoked wheels offered as an extra and on the fancier versions. You can also get a larger tank, full touring gear, five speeds forward, and a 1200cc XL engine.

With the basic XLH, you get one instrument.

it helped put the factory and the dealer into the black.

None of this would matter worth warm spit except for the true bottom line, the XLH's merits as a motorcycle. There was a recall for shifting, taken care of quickly, and one for the cast-alloy wheels, also done with dispatch and concern.

Given a place to stand, so to speak, each buyer could make the XLH his or her very own. (I put the double gender in here because my wife has a Sportster, okay?)

Chapter 24

FXRS Sport

The Best Bike Harley's Ever Made

Low profile and tapering solo seat give the FXRS Sport more of a cafe racer look than the XLCR ever had. Owner: Bruce Fischer, Irvine, California.

Driving north on California One, the scenic and twisting coastal route, I see lights in my truck's mirrors and "Whaaa, Whaaaaa" comes the shriek of two inline fours wound to the max. Tucked in close and ready to pounce comes "BRRRAAAAAAA," that wonderful staccato bark of the big twin on full song, the iron horse ridden with nerves of steel, and I think . . .

. . . By Damn Right! Harley-Davidson is back in the motorcycle business.

Which calls for an explanation. We've spent several pages discussing and examining ninety years of motorcycle history: rise and fall and rise again, technical brilliance and marketing skill, and a few lucky breaks. We've watched H-D born and reborn, into the right hands and into the black. How then, at this point, can I herald a return to the making of motorcycles?

With some trepidation, is how. First, when I was a magazine editor my basic rule was, don't make fun of anybody's scooter. It's a free market, different folks need different strokes and all that, and if it makes you happy to ride a machine I wouldn't have in my garage, okay. That's why we park in different garages.

Second, as I stated early on, when this book was being formed I polled the experts, the historians and restorers and builders and dealers, and asked them all for nominations.

Then I did the computation and weighed various values and used some but not all of my own views and made the selections you've seen here, assuming you didn't skip right to the chapter on your own bike, which is what I would have done myself.

Thing is, the views of the various experts are sort of like overlapping circles, with factors in common but not always a common sense of scale. All the judges like motorcycles and know about Harleys, but the collector has a different outlook than the designer does. All the viewpoints are valid. But they aren't the same.

And they aren't the only valid viewpoints. So, once I had the complete list and it didn't include the FXRS Sport, I added the Sport to the list. I don't care if the man on the street or in front of the cafe would rather look at old-style front ends or suspensions that pretend to be less effective than they are. The Sport deserves to be mentioned. In fact, I'd go so far as to say it's the best bike Harley ever made.

So we begin here with recent history. When the Harley engineers designed the FLT, with its unique front end and rubber engine mounts and new gearbox and so forth, they thought they'd follow with a more basic model, smaller and with less bodywork and ornamentation. But the bare bike looked odd minus panels, and the reverse-

steering stem-stanchion tube front suspension wasn't needed on the lighter model.

The lighter model became the newer and better model, with a frame of its own that was five times stiffer in torsion than the old FX frame was. Giving the game away here, the new frame got the rubber engine mounts, the five-speed gearbox, and the belt final drive of the FLT, but with a lighter front end, shared with the XL: The original official designation was Super Glide II, although that was quickly dropped for the letters FXR, R for rubber mount and to distinguish between the new FX and the older version, which kept the old frame and solid mounts. Both used the 80ci Shovelhead until the arrival of the Evolution engine.

The FXR was an immediate hit when it arrived in 1982 and the model began its own form of evolution. As can be seen from adjacent chapters, the marketeers and designers at H-D were having a grand time with style: Wide Glides and Disc Glides and Softails and so forth. They did well in sales, but one has to admit that they enhanced form at the expense of function.

Cast alloy wheels allow tubeless tires, which run cooler, lose pressure slower, and allow use of high-speed tires.

Compact air cleaner spells out the legend.

Next page
Belt drive is clean and quiet and you don't get lube all over the back of your jacket anymore.

The FXR, though, went the other way. There was no fussing with the past. Instead the FXRs got a police package and a touring package, neatly tucked bags, and conventional fairing. These were Harleys for people who wanted to ride motorcycles.

But the surprise benefit occurred in 1984. The sales department has always relished low seat heights, never mind that the width of the seat and the position of the pedals and controls can make a bike seem higher or lower than the static measurement implies. In 1984, the suspension, and thus the entire machine, was lowered by an inch and some. To keep the parts off the pavement, the suspension was made stiffer. The ride suffered, so did handling. Management is good at taking notes, so for 1985 there came an option, a sport package consisting of suspension that was raised back to the original position, plus a second disc brake in front, all for the miserly sum of $150.

Perhaps the option was an experiment, or a sop to the critics. The first version didn't even have its own name or initials, which if you know Harley comes as a surprise. (In fairness, note that they'd already used the word Sport for the touring version of the Super Glide, which they did because they'd already used Touring for the FLT.)

In any event, the improved suspension and brakes became the Sport option, as it's known to this day.

So all right, why is the FXRS Sport the best motorcycle Harley-Davidson has ever made?

Because it's a rider's bike, an evolved, functional, contemporary machine.

Harley-Davidson has never exactly coasted along. There have been times in The Motor Company's history when not all that was known was used. But they've always known. And they've been able to adapt and take advantage of hot irons, you could say, witness the revival of the old leading-link front suspension.

The Sport, though, uses everything that's been learned, at home and abroad. The electrics are chipped, moduled, and electronicked. There are suspension and carburetion from Japan, because the parts are excellent and the suppliers wanted the business: H-D management says a dismaying number of domestic companies don't want to bother with the mere 50,000 or so annual units represented by Harley-Davidson as a customer.

Ignition switch is aft of the rider's left leg. Chrome cover is for the ignition coil.

The Sport comes only with good, sporting tires. The wheels are disc and the tubes are missing, thank goodness. There are plenty of brakes and the tank is large enough either for touring or a day in the country. The seat fits most anybody, and the controls don't seem like such a stretch once you're up to speed.

Speaking of that, the V2 engine is truly state of the art, meaning it's normal, what most any company would do if they used a two-valve, overhead-valve, air-cooled engine. One might add here, why not? The big twin doesn't have the sheer speed or power of the one-liter fours, but it will pull hard out of the turns and run all day at

The FXRS is a large motorcycle, in terms of wheelbase and weight, but it's trim and balanced: the faster you go, the less bulk it seems to have.

Next page
And if you don't heed air cleaner's label, the tank of nitrous oxide, an oxygen-bearing compound and a whole stable of extra horses in a bottle, lets challengers know this isn't a machine to be trifled with.

189

rates one doesn't mention in a publication sold to impressionable youth. The Harley gets its power from displacement rather than revs, the aircraft principle rather than race class logic.

And it works. Not only does the V2 perform well, it's delivered in a mild state of tune, translated here into *more power.*

Our example isn't stock. You knew that. You knew that as soon as you looked at the right side of the beast and noted the big bottle of—gasp!—nitrous oxide; squeeze, in the street racer's vernacular.

The street racing Sport is presented here because that's now how it's done. The Sport lends itself to boring and stroking and hot cams, big carbs, tuned exhausts, and all the other wonders developed since 1903—the better to make motorcycles do what they are supposed to do, that is, cover ground in efficient and speedy fashion and yeah, make the riders whoop and grin while they do it.

A couple years ago, certain motorcycle companies began turning out imitation choppers. This came at a time when there was friction between the fanciers of the imported and the domestic machines, and there were people on both sides who made rude remarks. But during that time I rode a Kawasaki four into a lunch stop packed with Hell's Angels and got no static, and I used to visit the local sports bar with my dirt bike and nobody minded that either. So I concluded that it wasn't the difference between high or low bars, kicked-out or tucked-in front suspensions, it was simply honest machines versus posers.

That's harsh. Admittedly so, and I suspect there will be those who take offense.

So, do it. When Harley met the Davidsons, the founders began their project because they wanted to ride good motorcycles. They did their best, used the newest techniques, went back to school even. H and D prospered and dominated and later survived because of this basic, honest approach. The sturdy, unstressed, carefully planned big single did the job, while fancier or flashier or more radical rivals live now only in the index.

The FXRS-SP is the heir to that tradition. Harley-Davidson hasn't forgotten why they are here, which is why we're here, too.

Check this, and look again at
that 1909 Single: Machines run
in the family.

Index